CHEER UP YOUR WIFE

A DIY Biblical Guide

Copyright © 2012—Aleathea Dupree

All rights reserved. This book is protected by the copyright laws of the United States of America. This book may not be copied or reprinted for commercial gain or profit. The use of short quotations or occasional page copying for personal or group study is permitted and encouraged. Permission will be granted upon request.

Unless otherwise identified, Scripture quotations are from the Holy Bible, King James Version. Scripture quotations marked MSG are taken from The Message. Copyright © by Eugene H. Peterson 1993, 1994, 1995, 1996, 2000, 2001, 2002. Used by permission of NavPress Publishing Group. Scripture quotations marked NIV are taken from the Holy Bible, New International Version®. Copyright © 1973, 1978, 1984, 2011 by Biblica, Inc.™ Used by permission of Zondervan. All rights reserved worldwide. Scripture quotations marked AMP are taken from the Amplified ® Bible. Copyright © 1954, 1958, 1962, 1964, 1965, 1987 by The Lockman Foundation. Used by permission. Scripture quotations marked NKJV are taken from the New King James Version®. Copyright © 1982 by Thomas Nelson, Inc. Used by permission. All rights reserved. Scripture quotations marked NCV taken from the New Century Version®. Copyright © 2005 by Thomas Nelson, Inc. Used by permission. All rights reserved. Scripture quotations marked NASB are taken from the New American Standard Bible®. Copyright © 1960, 1962, 1963, 1968, 1971, 1972, 1973, 1975, 1977, 1995 by The Lockman Foundation. Used by permission. Scripture quotations marked ESV are taken from The Holy Bible, English Standard Version®. Copyright © 2001 by Crossway, a publishing ministry of Good News Publishers. Used by permission. All rights reserved. Scriptures marked NLT are taken from the New Living Translation. Copyright © 1996, 2004, 2007 by Tyndale House Foundation. Used by permission. All rights reserved.

ISBN-13: 978-0-9712-2401-8
ISBN-10: 0-9712-2401-3
Printed in the United States of America.

To order copies of this book, please email sales@dathea.com or visit www.cheerupyourwife.info.

CHEER UP YOUR WIFE

A DIY Biblical Guide

ALEATHEA DUPREE

DEDICATION

I dedicate this book to every man who desires to be the husband of a happy wife.

CONTENTS

Introduction   9

1. God's Dowry   13
2. Zipporah's Sisters   25
3. How Does Your Garden Grow?   47
4. Yours, Mine And IRS   57
5. Baby Mama Drama   69
6. Pillow Talk   83

Appendices

1. When A Husband Lies   95
2. Wound Care: Dealing With The Aftermath Of The Lie   99

INTRODUCTION

When a man hath taken a new wife, he shall not go out to war, neither shall he be charged with any business: but he shall be free at home one year, and shall cheer up his wife which he hath taken.

A newly married man must not be drafted into the army or be given any other official responsibilities. He must be free to spend one year at home, bringing happiness to the wife he has married.
(Deuteronomy 24:5 KJV and NLT)

It is said that it takes only twenty-one days to form a habit. If this is true, imagine what three hundred and sixty-five days of concentrated effort would do. Suppose every husband made a commitment to invest or re-invest one entire year in his marriage, and for each day of that year to do just one meaningful thing that would make his wife happy. Do you know what would happen? Our marriages would be restored, refreshed and revolutionized!

God — the Creator of marriage, the One who wrote the marital guidelines, and the only One who knows everything about everything — has said that the happiness of the wife, particularly a new wife, should be the priority of every husband. The instruction to "cheer up his wife" was not a suggestion from God: it was a mandate. Interestingly enough, this mandate was given immediately after the first mention of divorce in the Bible (see Deuteronomy 24:1). Could it be that God was giving us a preemptive strategy to avoid the problem of divorce? I believe so.

From the moment God issued this mandate, it became possible to accomplish. The fact that there so many disappointed, disgruntled, dissatisfied and just plain unhappy wives is an indication that there are husbands who are ignorant of this mandate and the significance of it, or they are ignoring it, or they have forgotten it.

Of course, in our day and time, there are not many husbands who are able to take a year off from work and other duties to stay at home just to cheer up their wives, but that is not the point. The point is that in the heart and mind of God, the happiness of the wife is a foundational priority of the marriage. There is something that God is expecting to see established in each marriage. He wants to see a reflection of Himself and His relationship with us, and the happiness of the wife is His gauge for measuring whether or not that expectation has been realized. In other words, when God wants to know what's going on in the marriage, He looks at the wife. She is the heart and true reflection of what is really going on in the marriage.

If cheering up a wife is that important to God that He would instruct a husband to focus one entire year doing just that, it should be that important to us. Only the most spectacular harvest would require such an investment of time and precious seed. Only the most magnificent of structures would require an entire year just to lay a foundation. Such effort is intended to produce the most abundant and glorious results, and such results is what God intends for our marriages. St. Augustine said, "The higher your structure is to be, the deeper must be its foundation." Laying a good, solid, deep foundation in marriage takes time and effort, but it is time and effort well spent.

Perhaps there are some husbands who are reading this and

Introduction

thinking, "Well, what about the husband's happiness?" I assure you that God is absolutely concerned about your happiness, but, if you feel the need to ask such a question, you may already have an unhappy wife. If that is the case, because you are the designated leader in your marriage, you may find that you are probably not very happy yourself. The state or conditions you lead your wife into will be the state or conditions in which you find yourself. You cannot lead your wife into happiness and not get there yourself. Therefore, the desire for your wife's happiness should motivate you, not offend you. No husband who desires to walk in obedience to God wants an unhappy wife, and no wife who desires to walk in obedience to God wants a frustrated man who feels like he's failing as a husband.

If you are a wife who is disappointed, disgruntled, dissatisfied and just plain unhappy, hope is on the way! If you are a husband married to such a wife, help is on the way! If you are single desirous of marriage, or already married and don't want to end up in either of the above categories, pay attention! This book is an encouragement, a challenge and a call to commitment to lay, repair, and strengthen the foundations of our marriages by looking at practical ways to carry out God's mandate to "cheer up your wife."

1

GOD'S DOWRY

He who finds a wife finds what is good and receives favor from the LORD. (Proverbs 18:22 NIV)

There are two kinds of husbands in this world: those who recognize and celebrate the true value of their wives, and those who do not. The husbands who recognize and celebrate the value of their wives reap a harvest of perpetual wealth and abundant blessings in their marriages. The husbands who fail to recognize and celebrate the true value of their wives rob themselves of the riches of the full benefits God intends when He blesses a man with a wife. Regardless of a husband's response or recognition, there is something of tremendous value that God gives to every wife: He gives her a dowry of divine favor.

Traditionally, a dowry is something of great value that is provided by a father for his daughter to bring with her into marriage. The purpose of the dowry is to help the husband take proper care of his wife, and to protect the wife against ill treatment by her husband. In the same way, when one of God's daughters marries, God provides a divine dowry of special favor that she brings with her into the marriage. This divine dowry of special favor positions the husband and provides him with the opportunity to obtain preferential treatment and special regard from God because of his wife.

The unmarried man is not the beneficiary of this particular kind of favor: it is reserved for the man who "finds a wife." Since this special favor is only available to the man who takes a wife, evidently, it is favor that God knows he needs in order to have good success in his role as a husband. This special favor is a gift — a special grace — from God to put the husband in the most advantageous position to take care of his wife and make progress in his marriage.

The key to the husband receiving this special favor is in understanding that this gift is a wellspring that God allows to flow through the wife. The key to releasing the flow of this favor lies in how the husband treats his wife. The more favorably the husband treats his wife, the more this special favor flows into the marriage. Conversely, the less favorably the husband treats his wife, the less divine preferential treatment or special regard he receives.

The husband must receive this favor, or more accurately, obtain it, which implies that it will require some effort on his part to draw it out. This favor does not just come with the wife and work on the husband's behalf no matter how he treats her. It's a flow. It flows out of and through her life into her husband's life to bless him and to help him. Because it is a flow, it can be dammed up or pumped up. If the husband treats his wife well, this special

God's Dowry

favor of God will flow freely, but if the husband mistreats his wife, he will block the flow and that favor will not work for him. As a matter of fact, it can even work against him.

To see how the favor a wife brings can work against a husband, consider the following two passages spoken directly to husbands in Malachi 2:13-14 and 1 Peter 3:7:

> And this you do with double guilt; you cover the altar of the Lord with tears [shed by your unoffending wives, divorced by you that you might take heathen wives], and with [your own] weeping and crying out because *the Lord does not regard your offering any more or accept it with favor at your hand* [emphasis added].
>
> Yet you ask, Why does He reject it? Because the Lord was witness [to the covenant made at your marriage] between you and the wife of your youth, *against whom you have dealt treacherously and to whom you were faithless* [emphasis added]. Yet she is your companion and the wife of your covenant [made by your marriage vows]. (Malachi 2:13-14 AMP)

In this passage in Malachi, these husbands placed themselves in a position of God's displeasure because they had "dealt treacherously" towards their wives. Treachery in marriage (which God hates), particularly on the husband's part, often results in divorce (which God also hates). I believe that every marriage that ends in divorce can be traced back to treacherous dealings within the marriage. Suffice it to say, dealing treacherously is a major favor

Cheer Up Your Wife

blocker.

The word *treacherous* means to be:

Deceptive: leading someone to believe what is not true; giving a false impression

Faithless: not adhering to allegiance, promises, vows, or duty; ready to betray trust; traitorous

Untrustworthy: not deserving of trust or confidence; undependable; unreliable

Dangerous: causing danger; perilous; risky; hazardous; unsafe; able or likely to cause physical injury

Unstable: unsteady; likely to sway; wavering; unsettled; easily moved, shaken or overthrown

The favor that the wife brings into the marriage gives the husband an opportunity to gain special regard from God. However, if the husband acts treacherously towards his wife in any of the above ways, God says He will "not regard" the husband when he comes before Him. God provides us with additional insight as He repeats this thought in 1 Peter 3:7 (AMP):

> In the same way you married men should *live considerately with [your wives]*, with an *intelligent recognition [of the marriage relation]* [emphasis added], honoring the woman as [physically] the weaker, but [realizing that you] are joint heirs of the grace (God's unmerited favor) of life, *in order that your prayers may not be hindered and cut off. [Otherwise you cannot pray*

effectively.] [emphasis added]

What is the significance of the husband's offering or prayers being hindered and cut off? Our offerings and prayers to God are not for God's benefit, they are for our benefit so that we can receive from Him the answers we need and the blessings He wants to pour into our lives. In both passages (Malachi 2:13-14 and 1 Peter 3:7), the husband is held responsible for the treatment of his wife, and in both instances, the husband's ability to receive from God is hindered and cut off if he mistreats his wife.

What's A Husband To Do?

In the passage in Malachi, God (implicitly) tells the husband what to do: don't deal treacherously with your wife. Cross any acts of treachery off your to-do list. If you have been deceptive, start being honest. I'm not talking here about confessing your wrong doings: I'm talking about replacing any intent to deceive with honesty. When a husband lies[1] he sows distrust, disrespect and insecurity into his marriage, and he will surely reap it. Don't lie to your wife in word, deed or intent. Instead, be intentionally honest.

If you have been faithless, start letting your yes be yes, and your no be no. When you exercise faith and move in confidence in what God has said, you will provide the kind of security God wants her to have. Be a man of your word; honor your vows; keep the promises you've made, and only make promises that you will keep. Become a testimony of faithfulness to your God, to your wife and to your marriage, not only with your words but also with your heart and your actions.

Cheer Up Your Wife

If you've been untrustworthy, you must establish a new pattern, over time, of trustworthiness by doing what you said you would do and not doing what you said you would not do. Consistency is the key. You develop untrustworthiness by being consistent in bad behavior. The way to establish trustworthiness is to be consistent in your good behavior.

Abusers are dangerous, but they are not the only ones who pose a threat in a marriage. Whenever a husband robs his wife of the security of a safe relationship in any way or leads her into unsafe situations (e.g. financially, sexually, spiritually), he creates a dangerous, risky, hazardous environment. In the areas where you may have created an insecure environment (i.e. physically, emotionally, financially, sexually, spiritually), do what needs to be done to create an atmosphere of safety for your wife.

As a husband, you have been placed in a God-given position of leadership. Even though many husbands lack godly examples of leadership that teach and show them how to be godly husbands, Christ remains the example of leadership that every husband must follow. Increase your knowledge of Him, and you will know how to lead well.

Christ carefully and diligently built His relationship with the Church, and He expects every husband to exercise the same care and diligence in building up his relationship with his wife. The Bible tells us that God has made everything available to you that you need for life and godliness (see 2 Peter 1:3). Therefore, He has made available to you everything you need to be the leader in your marriage. If you have been unstable, you can begin to lead your wife with confidence and integrity. Obedience to God will cause you to walk in integrity before Him and before your wife.

Ask yourself if you have committed any of these treacherous acts. Look carefully and prayerfully at the list of treacherous acts above and examine your heart. Are any of these things there? Are any of these treacherous traits showing up in your life and marriage? Be honest with yourself about it. One sure way to check if the favor flow has been blocked is to examine your life and circumstances. Are you progressing in life the way you should? Are you moving forward and upward, or does your life and ministry seem stagnated? Are you receiving answers to prayers and consistently seeing the blessings of God in your life? And here's the million-dollar question: *is your wife happy*? If your wife is not happy, that's a sure sign that something on the treacherous hit list may have reared its ugly head in your marriage.

Ask your wife if she sees any of these things in you or in your relationship. Sometimes we are blind to our own faults, or we see only what we want to see. Your wife is like a mirror in your life: she will reflect back to you the image you present to her. If you don't like what she's been reflecting back at you, check what you have been presenting to her. If you think yourself innocent of these things and she does not, you've got a major problem in your marriage that needs to be addressed.

If when you ask her she points out anything on the treacherous hit list, whether you believe it or not, or whether you see it or not, give attention to it. The Bible says that when you realize you have offended your brother, you must go to him and make peace (see Matthew 5:23-24). Making peace is not the same as talking peace, and an apology demonstrated is much more effective than an apology simply stated. When your wife sees you making changes, she will know that you have heard her. If your wife doesn't feel heard by you, she may become like the wives spoken of in Malachi covering the altar of the Lord with her tears. It's better for her to be able to talk to you (and be heard) than for her to feel that she has to talk to God about you. If she cries out in prayer against you, the attention you want from God in prayer will be redirected to attending to her cries.

Ask God to search your heart and to show you anything that might be blocking the flow of His favor in your life. The Psalmist said:

> Search me [thoroughly], O God, and know my heart! Try me and know my thoughts! And see if there is any wicked or hurtful way in me, and lead me in the way everlasting. (Psalm 139:23, 24 AMP)

God will surely answer such a prayer, not so you can feel condemned or guilty, but so you can unblock the blessings that He wants to pour into your life. Please keep in mind that when God answers and shows you what's really in your heart, He may very well do so through your wife.

Not only does God want you to eliminate treachery from your life, the passage in 1 Peter 3:7 also tells you something else that God wants you to do: be considerate of your wife. Husbands, major in your wife. Most husbands are with their wives almost every day of the year for several hours throughout the day. If you can be considered expert in a subject after a few hours of study each week over a relatively short period of time, how much more should every husband be an expert on his wife. There should be no one on earth that takes a greater interest in her than you. There should be no one else on this earth (other than her) who knows more about your wife than you do.

There are things you can know about her by observation: study your wife. What does she like? What makes her heart rejoice? What makes her feel secure? What makes her feel satisfied? What makes her feel loved and appreciated? What makes her happy? These are things you should know and focus on. Find out what's important to her and let those things be important to you. This is how you will be able to live considerately with her.

There are other things you can know by interrogation: ask your wife. Don't presume or assume anything: ask. And when you ask, listen to what she says. Put your ego in neutral and really hear what she's saying without trying to excuse or defend yourself. There is no need to take offense if you realize that by communicating her heart to you she is expressing a level of confidence in your ability to be the husband she wants and needs you to be.

Some things you can only know by revelation: ask God about your wife. Don't spend your time simply trying to avoid the things she doesn't like: that's not enough. Being considerate of your wife is more than just trying to appease her. Consideration involves understanding. If you do not understand her, how can you live with her in an understanding way? Wisdom is the prerequisite of understanding: not the wisdom of the world that says a man can't ever understand a woman, but the wisdom of God. In James 1:5, God says if you need wisdom, just ask Him and He'll give it to you liberally! Ask God daily to give you wisdom in understanding your wife and being considerate of her.

The Bible tells us that a man's gift will make room for him and bring him before great men (Proverbs 18:16). The special favor that God provides through your wife is one such gift. Prove yourself faithful and responsible by not dealing treacherously with her and being considerate of her, and you will be positioned to receive the King's favor. Celebrate and cherish that gift and God's favor will flow into your life and marriage like a never-ending river! Always remember that a marriage in which a husband devalues the divine dowry of favor is a marriage that cannot reach its maximum potential.

A Word to the Wives

Just as water cannot flow through a pipe without getting it wet, in the same way, God's favor cannot flow through you without blessing your life. Never forget that the King has provided favor because of you. You are the vessel He has chosen to honor and through whom He pours out this special favor. At the same time, remember that it is not your favor: it is God's favor, so make sure that there is nothing in you that would block the flow to you and through you. Keep your heart clear and God's favor will work for you whether your husband takes advantage of it or not.

Even if you are mistreated, commit yourself to God and continue to do good (see 1 Peter 4:19). Refuse to be defiled by lingering anger, unforgiveness and bitterness. Forgive all the time, every time, because that is what God is requiring of you (see Matthew 18:21, 22; Ephesians 4:32).[2] If your husband has not yet reached the point where he appreciates and celebrates your value, don't allow that to diminish who you are. Never forget that you are the King's daughter and even if your husband is not listening to your heart, your Heavenly Father is.

Your desire should be that your husband receives the favor of God. If you don't have that desire, ask God to give it to you. Pray that your husband will be humble and quick to agree with God about any acts of treachery. Pray that his heart will be tender toward the voice of the Lord and toward you.

Endnotes

1. See Appendix 1, *When A Husband Lies*
2. See Appendix 2, *Wound Care: Dealing With The Aftermath Of A Lie*

2

ZIPPORAH'S SISTERS

Submitting yourselves one to another in the fear of God. Wives, submit yourselves unto your own husbands, as unto the Lord. (Ephesians 5:21-22 KJV)

Being a godly husband has its challenges, but from the moment a Christian man declares his marriage vows and enters into covenant with the God who established marriage, all of the resources necessary to equip the husband to be the servant-leader and head of his wife are made available to him. We have spoken previously about the divine dowry of favor that a wife brings into the marriage which is a major resource to her husband. Let us discuss another resource in marriage: submission.

For many wives, submission is not a favorite topic. Sometimes, for the husbands of those same wives, submission is *too* favorite a topic. In many cases, this disparity is due to a lack of understanding on both sides of what submission is really about.

Cheer Up Your Wife

Submission that is carried out the way God intended brings order, freedom and unity into a marriage. However, misunderstood or applied incorrectly, chaos, bondage and disunity result.

Submission in marriage is also important for a single person to understand because it helps him/her to recognize crucial qualities in a potential mate, and to understand what will be required of both the husband and wife in marriage. It's especially important that husbands and wives understand the voluntary nature of the submission called for in marriage; otherwise, it will be misunderstood, misused or not put into practice at all.

Let's begin with a working definition of what it means to submit. The word *submit* is derived from the Greek word *hupotasso* which is a combination of two Greek words: *hupo* which means "under" and *tasso* which means "to arrange in an orderly fashion." Using those two definitions, to submit means "to arrange in an orderly fashion under." One of the interesting things about the word *hupotasso* is that it is a military term that refers to the arranging of troops in a military fashion under the command of a leader in order to carry out effective warfare.

In marriage, God has ordained that the husband represents the Head (Christ), and the wife represents the Body (the Church). This is God's divine order. He says, in effect, "Wife, I want you to arrange yourself under the headship of your husband for a good and proper purpose." That's submission. The problem most people, particularly wives, have with the idea of submission is that they interpret it as inequality.

Submission Is Not Inequality

We hear the word "under" and we tend to think in terms of hierarchy or in terms of the one who is under being inferior or less important than the head. This is not the case in biblical submission which should not be thought of in terms of "under" and "above," but in terms of leading and following. Submission does not mean inequality: it means that the husband and wife are equal in status but different in roles or function. Submission works best when both spouses understand that the wife is not inferior to her husband, and the husband is not superior to his wife. Let us examine how God set up the marital relationship from the beginning.

In Genesis 2:18, the LORD God said, "It is not good that the man should be alone; I will make him an *help meet* for him. [emphasis added]" The wife is given by God as a "help meet" an *ezer kenegdo* to her husband. The traditional teaching concerning the woman as help meet sometimes portrays her as a type of assistant or helper somewhat inferior or of less importance to the one being helped. But, if you examine the context of the use of the word *ezer* in the scripture,[1] you will see that the word refers to either God or military allies. In these instances, the one giving the help is superior to the one receiving the help. If God had said I will make an *ezer* for the man, He would have been saying that the wife, the one giving help, is superior to the husband... but, He did not say that.

God did not want inequality in the marriage so he added the word *kenegdo* (meet) which changes the meaning to that of "equal rather than superior status." So the wife, as the *ezer kenegdo* (or help meet), is one who is the same as the other and who surrounds, protects, aids, helps, and supports. From the very beginning, God ordains that the husband and wife be equal in status but different in roles or function.

When God speaks of *hupotasso* or submission in marriage, He's talking about two people who are absolutely equal in His eyes. There is not a level of inferiority of one to the other. When a woman marries, she is (knowingly or unknowingly) making a choice to place herself, an equal, under the headship of another equal, her husband, in order that there can be order and function in the family.

Ephesians 5:23 tells us that the husband is the "head" of the wife. In the Greek, there are two different and distinct words that are translated "head." The first is *arche* which is used to denote "first" in terms of importance and power (we use it in such words as archangel, archbishop, archenemy). It also means "ruler." Paul did not use the word *arche* when he spoke of the husband being the head. This lets us know that in God's eyes, the husband is not first in terms of importance and power, and he is not the ruler of his wife.

Instead of the word *arche* Paul used the word *kephale*. This word means "head" as in the part of one's body; it was also used to mean "foremost" in terms of position. It was never used to mean leader or boss or chief or ruler. *Kephale* is also a military term that means "one who leads" but not in the sense of a director. A director sits back and gives instructions, commands or tasks for someone else to follow or carry out but does not get fully involved or lead in the doing of those things. A husband who functions as a director is not fulfilling the biblical mandate of headship as it relates to submission. The husband must be the *kephale* — one who goes before the troops — not someone who orders the troops from a safe distance. The *kephale* is the leader in the sense of being in the lead, or in military terminology, he is the first one into battle. The husband is not the ruler or the boss or the chief of his wife; he is not first in terms of importance and power; he is not the leader in the sense of one who gives out orders for his wife to follow. The husband is in the lead position. In other words, the husband is to lead by example.

Christ says, "Follow Me," sets the example, and then leaves the following up to us. With regards to submission in marriage, the husband must set the example of submission for the wife to follow. Jesus said, "For I have given you an example, that ye should do as I have done to you." (John 13:15). This is the biblical model of submission. Jesus is equally God, yet He voluntarily placed Himself in submission to the Father. He did not regard submission as a threat to the equality that He knew existed between Himself and the Father. In marriage, submission should not be viewed as a threat to equality either.

Submission Is Not Servitude

The submission of a wife to her husband is a gift she gives to him, not something the husband demands. Submission in marriage is a voluntary act. Submission cannot be forced; it must be done willingly. Forced submission is slavery, and Christ came to set us free not to enslave us. A slave may perform the work the master desires but resent every command given. This is not submission. True submission is done with a willing spirit. The husband represents Christ. Therefore, as the representative of Christ, the husband cannot demand submission of his wife or force her to submit because Christ does not demand submission of us, neither does He force us to submit to Him.

Submission Is Not Ignorance

A submitted wife should be an informed wife. In John 15:15 (AMP) Jesus said:

> I do not call you servants (slaves) any longer, for the servant does not know what his master is doing (working out [The Message translation says, "thinking about/planning"]). But *I have called you My friends, because I have made known to you everything that I have heard from My Father* [emphasis added]. [I have revealed to you everything that I have learned from Him.]

Jesus said, everything the Father tells Me, I tell you. Everything the Father reveals to Me, I reveal to you. Everything I learn from Him, I teach you. I don't just tell you the *what*, I tell you the *why*. He says, the difference between a servant and a friend is that a servant is not told what's going on, but a friend is told everything. In the same way, the husband as the head of his wife should be communicating his goals, plans and strategies to his wife. And in doing so, he should not just be communicating the what, but he should also communicate the why. If he does not communicate with his wife, he will paralyze his marriage.

Paralysis is a loss or impairment of voluntary movement in a body part, or loss of sensation over a region of the body. When a husband fails to communicate with his wife what his thoughts and plans are and what revelation and instruction he is receiving from God, he is not treating her as a friend but as a slave, and loss of voluntary movement and/or loss of sensation in the marriage will be the result. In a paralyzed marriage, critical communication is lacking. The wife no longer voluntarily helps the husband to move forward because she is not "on board" with his plans. The husband, feeling a lack of support, becomes resentful towards his wife. She, on the other hand, feels left out of the loop, and as a result, she becomes resentful towards him. The marriage is paralyzed. Physically speaking, the cure for paralysis is communication. There must be unhindered effective communication from the head to the body. Likewise, in marriage there must be unhindered effective communication from the husband to the wife concerning his thoughts, plans, strategies and revelations.

Being submitted does not mean that you don't have a right to ask questions. Even God says that if you call to Him He will answer you and tell you great and unsearchable things that you do not know (see Jeremiah 33:3). A wife has a right to know the reasoning behind an instruction, direction, or decision, and if the husband does not communicate his thoughts or plans, the wife has a right to ask about what's going on and receive an answer. Submission does not mean that you don't discuss things with one another: it means that you do.

Submission Is Not Obedience

Cheer Up Your Wife

Submission is not inequality; submission is not servitude; submission is not ignorance; and submission is not obedience. There is a difference between submission and obedience. To obey simply means to follow a command; to conform; or to comply with an order whether you want to or not. Submission, on the other hand, implies that you *want* to. A wife is not required to obey her husband. She is not a child and she is not a slave. The word used for submission (*hupotasso*) is not the same as the word used for obey (*hupakouo*), which is a word that a parent might use regarding a child, or a master might use regarding a slave.

Some husbands treat their wives like children or like slaves. They talk to them and treat them as if they have no sense or ability, or as if they are inferiors with no rights. This is not biblical submission. Only children are commanded to obey in the family relationship:

> Children, obey your parents in the Lord: for this is right (Ephesians 6:1 NKJV)

> Children, obey your parents in all things: for this is well pleasing unto the Lord. (Colossians 3:20 NKJV)

Ultimately, we want our children to submit to godly authority because they realize it is the right thing to do and because they want to do the right thing. But whether they realize the rightness of it or not, while they are children, they are *required* to obey. A wife, however, is not a child and she is not to be treated like one.

Marriage is not a "do as you're told" relationship. The Bible says wives must be in submission to their own husbands; it does not say they are to obey their husbands. As was stated earlier, submission is voluntary. Your will is involved. You do it because you want to do it—you choose to do it—not because you're forced to do it. Biblical submission is something you do to yourself, not something someone does to you.

Sometimes in marriage, the problem is not with submission, but with a lack of leadership or headship. Ideally, the husband will recognize his role as one who leads by example, and he will step to the forefront shouldering his responsibilities. When the husband does not carry out his leadership role, sometimes the wife is left to shoulder responsibility that is not assigned to her. The result is a very unhappy wife. Such was the case with Zipporah (in Exodus 4:24-26):

> At a lodging place on the way, the LORD met Moses and was about to kill him. But Zipporah took a flint knife, cut off her son's foreskin and touched Moses' feet with it. "Surely you are a bridegroom of blood to me," she said. So the LORD let him alone. (At that time she said "bridegroom of blood," referring to circumcision.)

Zipporah may appear at first to be an unsubmissive wife based on how she reacts or responds to her husband. But, in actuality she was not. The problem here was not a lack of submission but a lack of leadership.

In reading this passage, we understand implicitly that God had given Moses the responsibility of circumcising his son; a responsibility that he had neglected to carry out. As a result, God was going to kill Moses. Zipporah was then faced with a heart-wrenching decision: she could stand back and watch her husband die for failing to carry out the commandment that God required, or she could carry out the bloody and painful task of circumcising her son herself and spare her husband's life. She chose the latter. The result was anger, frustration and bitter resentment for having to do what her husband should have done. The same is true today. When a wife feels forced to take on certain responsibilities because her husband has not done what he was supposed to do, anger, frustration, and bitter resentment are often the result, particularly when taking on such responsibilities causes her pain. There are some things a wife (whose husband is alive, well and able) should never have to do. There are too many wives whose hands are bloody because they've had to take on hard and difficult tasks that their husbands were commanded to do but neglected.

What's A Husband To Do?

In marriage there is equal status but differing roles and responsibilities. They are different but intrinsically connected and designed to work together for the common good of the marriage. You, husband, are the God-ordained leader, so you must be in the forefront when it comes to shouldering responsibilities in the marriage, be they spiritual, financial, parental or any other responsibility. When you married your wife, you took on the responsibility of seeing to her well-being and all that concerns her.

The best leaders recognize that they cannot do it all on their own so they utilize the best resources of those who they are leading. You must take responsibility for all that God requires of you as a husband, and you must also know when to delegate responsibility and take advantage of the resources available to you in your wife. When delegating responsibilities, you may want to keep these two cautionary guidelines in mind.

First, don't delegate to your wife that for which you are responsible to God for carrying out. Your assignment as the head is your assignment and your wife is not required to carry out your assignment. She has her own assignment. When God asks you about your assignment as a husband you will not be able to point to your wife and say, "I would have gotten it done but she didn't help me." You must carry out your responsibilities whether your wife helps you or not.

Secondly, don't delegate to your wife that for which she is neither physically, emotionally, or spiritually equipped nor prepared to handle. That means you will have to take the time to discover where your wife needs to be built up and where she is strong. Guard against your wife's weaknesses, and build up your wife's strengths and together, see how those strengths may be best utilized for the good of your marriage.

Zipporah was physically able to carry out Moses' responsibility to circumcise his son, but emotionally and spiritually she wasn't ready for it. This was a responsibility she should never have had to carry out. Husband, there are some things your wife should never have to do as long as you are alive, well and able. Make sure your wife's hands are not being bloodied because she is carrying out your responsibilities. Make sure she is not going through emotional turmoil because of things you are responsible for and have neglected to do. See to it that your wife's resources and giftedness as a person are being utilized and utilized correctly or she will end up frustrated. There has to be a balance between her submissiveness to you as her God-ordained head, and the proper and appropriate utilization of her strengths.

In marriage, there is plenty of room for manliness but no room for machismo. It will not make you any less manly to encourage your wife in an area where she is strong and you are not. If you know that you can't tell a Phillips screwdriver from a flathead screwdriver and your wife can, rather than frustrating yourself (and her), if she is so inclined, let *her* do the assembling while *you* read her the instructions. Help her to help you get the job done, and when she does get the job done, don't minimize what she has accomplished by having a bad attitude because she was able to do it and you weren't. Instead, thank her, give her a hug, and tell her "We make a great team!"

While there may be some things she can do better than you, there are other things with which she will struggle that you can do with relative ease. Take the time to discover what causes her to feel burdened and then do what you can to alleviate what might be a weight on her shoulders, particularly if the weight she's carrying is the burden of your responsibilities. Each wife is different. Some wives willingly take on certain of their husband's responsibilities because they want to. As long as it's not out of order and she's up to the task, go for it! Other wives take on certain responsibilities because they have to. They feel they have no choice because they see the need and want to make sure what needs to get done gets done. Make sure your wife is not in the have to category. If your wife, of necessity, takes on those responsibilities that you neglect, her respect for you may become clouded by resentment.

There are certain things the husband as the head of his wife is supposed to be doing. Ephesians 5:28-30 (KJV) says:

> Even so husbands should love their wives as their own bodies [New Living Translation says "For a man who loves his wife actually shows love for himself"]. He who loves his own wife loves himself. For no man ever hated his own flesh, but nourishes and carefully protects and cherishes it, as Christ does the church, because we are members (parts) of His body.

The husband as head must love his wife. "Love" here is the word *agapaó* which speaks of the God-kind of love; intense love that is based on evaluation and choice; an act of the will. This kind of love is a commitment that is not based on an emotional feeling. It's a sacrificial kind of love that seeks to do what is in the best interest of another desiring another's highest good. *Agapé* love describes the love God gives freely, sacrificially and unconditionally regardless of response. This kind of love is unconditional: this love is still given even if it's not received or returned. Agapé gives and gives and gives. It is not withheld. This is the way you are required to love your wife. You must love her when you feel like it and when you don't feel like it. You must love her whether she responds to you in a loving manner or not.

You may be tempted to think that it is not possible for you to love this way, but you have been equipped to do it. Romans 5:5 tells us that "God's love has been poured out in our hearts through

Cheer Up Your Wife

the Holy Spirit Who has been given to us." This kind of love is a supernatural love that is empowered by the Holy Spirit, and you have it in you. Love your wife by doing what's in her best interest. Love your wife by seeking her highest good. Love your wife enough not to allow her to carry the weight of your responsibilities.

The husband as head must nourish his wife. To nourish implies that not only should you be willing to be the breadwinner or provider to take care of your wife's physical needs, you should also be concerned with her emotional and spiritual needs; her overall growth. We are spirit, soul and body, and all three need to be nourished. See to it that your wife is being nourished spiritually. If you can't cook, get her to a place where she can enjoy the best meal. Your wife's spirit (as does yours) needs a regular diet of the Word of God. Even if you are a babe in Christ, seek out resources, godly teaching and pastorship that will enable the proper nourishment of the spirit. Your wife must be nourished emotionally. This means taking the time to understand her (as was discussed in the previous chapter). This means communication. Your wife's physical needs are your responsibility. Anything that the physical body requires for growth and well-being is what you must seek to provide. Malnourished is still nourished, but it is not the best. Go for the best!

The husband as head must cherish his wife. To cherish (*thalpō*) means the husband feels and shows affection for his wife; he protects her and cares lovingly for her. He recognizes her value and treats her as someone precious and valuable. Treat your wife like a friend not a servant. Share your plans, goals and strategies with her, and when you tell her the what, as much as possible, tell her the why. Treat her as an equal not as an inferior person.

Treating her as an equal does not mean treating her like a man. It means that you recognize her value as a human being, as your wife, and as Peter says, as a fellow heir (see 1 Peter 3:7).

So often we hear that the wife should provide a safe haven of rest for the husband, and that has its place. But, God didn't tell the wife to cherish the husband; He told the husband to cherish the wife. The literal meaning of the word *cherish* is "to keep warm" which suggests that it is the husband who is responsible for providing a secure, warm place for his wife. He is to provide a nest-home which pictures a place of security, a place of warmth and a place of nourishment. Too many husbands are content to die to their manhood and step aside and let the woman do "it," but the Bible encourages you to "Be on your guard; stand firm in the faith; be men of courage; be strong." (1 Corinthians 16:13). Don't look to your wife to provide that which God requires of you as a husband.

A Word To The Wives

Understand that submission is an act of faith. You submit as service to the Lord not as service to your husband. Your submission has everything to do with your relationship to God and what you know of Him, and the purpose that He is working out in your life. It's an act of faith. You submit to God under the headship of your husband trusting God's divine order.

Submission focuses on position, not on personality. Your submission is independent of your husband's submission. In other words, you should not say, "I'll submit if he does so and so." You submit whether he does "so and so" or not. Even if he is not obedient to the Word, you can still function in divine order. 1 Peter 3:1 (NASB) says:

> Wives, in the same way be submissive to your husbands so that, if any of them do not believe the word, they may be won over without words by the behavior of their wives

Your submissiveness is a soul-winning tool: it can attract your husband to your God. A husband does not have to be perfect in order for you to submit to him. A man at best is at best a man.

There is a tendency to focus so much on the "wives, submit yourselves to your own husbands..." verse (Ephesians 5:22) that we neglect the verse that comes before it which says, "submit yourselves to one another..." (Ephesians 5:21). That means that there should be a mutual recognition and utilization of authority, responsibility and resources. There will be some things that your husband may be able to do better, more effectively or more efficiently than you: let him. There will be some things that you will be able to do better, more effectively, or more efficiently than him. This is where your strengths may be utilized. While he may be your head in the sense that he is to be your covering, you are also his covering because you are his glory (see Proverbs 12:4 and 1 Corinthians 11:7). As a wife, you also have authority in the household (see an example of a wife with authority in Proverbs 31). You are co-laborers, joint heirs, team mates, and you are to manage your household together in joint cooperation.

What does this require? In large part, it requires an understanding of each other's strengths and weaknesses, needs and desires. That means you'll both need to communicate with one another. You need to be able to talk to your husband about how you feel—not how he's making you feel, but how you feel as a result of and in light of the things that are now happening or not happening within the marriage. This is not about blaming or accusing each other: it's about understanding one another.

You are your husband's helpmate. Let him know and help him to understand how you can be of help to him. At the same time, recognize that your way of doing things is not the only way. Talk together about what might be the best way to do things in a way that works for both of you and for the best management of your household. Your marriage is *your* marriage (i.e. you and your husband's), so you have to figure out together what works in your house.

Does being a submitted wife mean that you have to accept *anything* from your husband: any kind of treatment or behavior? Absolutely not! A submitted wife understands that she is empowered to say "No!" You need to say "No!" and say it in a way that your husband can hear and respect. That might mean counseling. That might mean going to the police. That might mean having another authority or person of respect intervene.

Some of you may be wondering, what if you are married to someone who instead of loving and nourishing and cherishing you does you harm or violence? What if your husband violates you physically (with domestic abuse) or sexually? What if he forbids or discourages you from doing what God says you should be doing? In those instances, you may need to break rank and let him know that you cannot submit to that kind of behavior. Remember, your husband may be your head, but God is the Commander in Chief, and you are ultimately responsible for doing what He says must be done above all else. If subjecting yourself results in performing some action that contradicts the clear teaching of Scripture (i.e. going against the will of God), you are to do what God wants. This is not an exception to submission: it is the ultimate submission. As Peter and the apostles said (in Acts 5:29), "We must obey God rather than men!"

Ask God to give you the desire to submit to His divine order with grace. Pray that your husband will grow in leadership skills in your relationship—nourishing you spiritually, emotionally, and physically; protecting and caring for you. Pray that he will lead you wisely and love you sacrificially, so that God will be glorified in your marriage. (Ephesians 5:25-33; Colossians 3:19)

A Final Word On Submission

The purpose of submission is unity/oneness.

> For we are members of His body, of His flesh, and of His bones. [see Gen. 2:24] For this cause shall a man leave his father and mother, and shall be joined unto his wife, *and they two shall be one flesh. This is a great mystery: but I speak concerning Christ and the church* [emphasis added]. (Ephesians 5:30-32 KJV)

Marriage is supposed to give a real life picture of the relationship between Christ and the church. The husband and wife are united for a common purpose. What is that purpose? Let us look at a portion of the prayer of the Lord Jesus Christ, the Head of the Church from John 17:11, 20-23 (KJV):

> 11 And now I am no more in the world, but these are in the world, and I come to thee. Holy Father, keep through thine own name those whom thou hast given me, that they may be one, as we are.
>
> 20 Neither pray I for these alone, but for them also which shall believe on me through their word; 21 That they all may be one; as thou, Father, art in me, and I in thee, that they also may be one in us: that the world may believe that thou hast sent me. 22 And the glory which thou gavest me I have given them; that they may be one, even as we are one: 23 I in them, and thou in me, that they may be made perfect in one [unity]; and that the world may know that thou hast sent me, and hast loved them, as thou hast loved me.

God desires oneness in the Body of Christ, and God desires oneness in marriage in particular so that the world will see a real life picture of how much He loves us. How does God accomplish this oneness? He accomplishes it through submission: the body must cooperate with the head, and the head must cooperate with the body. This unity between the head and the body (or the husband and the wife) is accomplished through submission.

A godly marriage in which the wife submits herself as a service to the Lord, and the husband loves his wife and is her head as Christ is the Head of the church, is the most powerful evangelistic tool. From the beginning, God has wanted a united front in marriage. He gave Adam a military ally in his wife so that they could stand together as a united front against the enemy. If Eve and Adam had stayed in unity, sin would have never entered the world. The enemy knew that as long as they stood together in unity, he wouldn't stand a chance. That's why he spoke to Eve individually instead of speaking to them both at the same time. He knew that if he could get the woman to get out from under God's divine order she could use her equal standing with her husband to persuade him to get out from under God's divine order as well. It worked with the first Adam but not with the second and last Adam, Jesus Christ. When Satan came to tempt Jesus in the wilderness, he used the same strategy: he tried to get Jesus to come out from under God's divine order. But every time Jesus said, "It is written..." He was really saying, I'm staying submitted to God, and the enemy was defeated.

When you arrange yourself according to God's divine order you will defeat the enemy every time. The moment you step out of God's order, you set yourself or your spouse in a position to be attacked by the devil. We don't have to fight the devil. We need only submit ourselves to God, resist the devil's attempts to get us to usurp divine order, and he will run from us in terror (see James 4:7).

The devil is not interested in attacking your marriage, but he is interested in attacking the purpose God has for marriage, which is to demonstrate, through mutual submission, God's love for the world leading us to salvation. Reflecting the love of God in Christ is God's ultimate goal in marriage and everything else. In order to accomplish this, we must line up under God's divine order and put submission in its proper place in marriage.

Endnotes

1. Scripture references for the Hebrew word *ezer* (help): Genesis 2:18, 20; Exodus 18:4; Deuteronomy 33:7, 26, 29; Psalm 20:2; 33:20; 70:5; 89:19; 115:9, 10, 11; 121:1, 2; 124:8; 146:5; Isaiah 30:5; Ezekiel 12:14; Daniel 11:34; Hosea 13:9

3

HOW DOES YOUR GARDEN GROW?

Do not withhold good from those to whom it is due, when it is in your power to do it. (Proverbs 3:27 ESV)

I'm a strong advocate for jealousy in marriage. Now that I have your attention, let me explain what I mean. Jealousy should be in every marriage, but only a certain kind of jealousy. There is an ungodly jealousy that is bred from insecurity that erodes trust in a marriage, and there is a godly jealousy that is bred from security that builds trust in a marriage. Too many Christian marriages (i.e. marriages between believing husbands and their believing wives) are suffering from ungodly jealousy.

God describes Himself as a jealous God. He even goes as far as to say, Jealous is His name (see Exodus 34:14). There is nothing wrong with godly jealousy, but ungodly jealousy is detrimental to any relationship. How do you know if you have godly or ungodly jealousy? The distinction is pretty simple: ungodly jealousy is jealous *of*; godly jealousy is jealous *over*.

Whenever you are threatened by, or envious of, what someone else has, and feel that it should be yours and not theirs,

Cheer Up Your Wife

that is ungodly jealousy. Ungodly jealousy wants that which rightfully belongs to someone else. When you are unable to celebrate the accomplishment, victory, advantage or blessing of someone else, ungodly jealousy is at work. There is nothing wrong with wanting good things to happen in your life. However, when you are unable to celebrate good things happening in the lives of other people, and feel that you should have what they have, you are in the clutches of ungodly jealousy. Ungodly jealousy in the life of a believer is what happens when you are deceived into thinking that God has denied you something that is good that you believe you have a right to have. Jealousy *of* is fear-based.

Godly jealousy, on the other hand, is love-based. Godly jealousy knows, celebrates, guards and protects what it has been given. It is jealous *over*. If you had been given a priceless diamond as a gift, would you be jealous when the light catches it and shows off the beauty of its facets? Would you cover it with mud to hide its brilliance so that no attention is drawn to it? When others see its beauty and "Oooh!" and "Aaah!" over it, would you resent their admiration? Of course you would not, because it's *your* gift! It was given to you for a blessing and for you to enjoy. So then, why would a husband be jealous of his wife? Why should he be jealous of the ministry God has blessed her with? Why should he be jealous of the blessings that the favor on her life attracts?

My engagement ring is a beautiful pear-shaped diamond. From time to time, I still get compliments on its eye-catching appearance. Even though I am the one wearing the ring, people look at it and comment on how much my husband must love me to have given me a ring like that. The beauty and brilliance that I,

How Does Your Garden Grow?

as his wife, display brings honor to him.

Proverbs 31:23 (NIV) says:

> Her husband is respected at the city gate, where he takes his seat among the elders of the land.

The husband is respected because of the beauty and noble character of his wife. Why then would a husband be jealous of the good things that his wife's favor and character attract or produce? The husband is intended to be a primary beneficiary of the favor on his wife's life. That favor is to be nurtured and cherished not abused or resented. The husband who is jealous of his wife will recognize the favor that is on her life but may try to use it to make himself look good. The husband who is jealous of his wife will celebrate the attention his wife gets, but then may try to use that attention for his own gain (sometimes at the wife's expense). The husband who is jealous of his wife will not encourage his wife's efforts privately, but when those same efforts afford him a place in the spotlight, he may be the first to "smile for the camera." These things ought not to be so.

The Bible says that the wife is the crown of the husband (see Proverbs 12:4); she is his glory (see 1 Corinthians 11:7). When a husband truly recognizes this, he will not have the need to compete with his wife for attention or recognition because he will understand that the more his wife shines, the more honor she brings to him.

Cheer Up Your Wife

What's A Husband To Do?

Celebrate your wife's success and advantage. When others recognize the favor in the person of your wife — whether it be displayed in her appearance, her giftedness, her skills or in any other way that favor is displayed — don't resent it. Instead, celebrate the grace of God that is on her life. When others praise your wife's virtues or accomplishments, don't be notably silent: be the first and the loudest to give her what is due. When your wife's favor brings her before great men and women, be the one she wants to escort her into their presence. When your wife does something well and with a spirit of excellence, do not withhold your praise or refuse to give credit where credit is due. Be generous with your compliments.

When I was investigating the church of which I am now a member, there were two tests that helped to confirm that it was the right place for me. First, I had to feel welcome there no matter how I dressed or looked. Secondly, I listened to hear and watched to see how the pastor would speak of and treat his wife. At my very first visit to the church, I did not have to guess who the pastor's wife was because he made her known. He spoke well of her publicly and privately. He praised her and declared the uniqueness of her position in his life. He refused to call her "First" Lady but insisted on referring to her as the *only* Lady, making it clear that there would be no others. That was seven years ago, and he declares it even more today. Gentlemen, don't praise your wife only in public when others are around: praise her privately also. Don't praise her only in private when no one else is around: praise her publicly. Praise her in the presence of her children. Praise her

How Does Your Garden Grow?

in the presence of other men. Praise her in the presence of other women. If you're a pastor, praise her from the pulpit.

The Bible says:

> Charm can be deceiving, and beauty fades away, but *a woman who honors the LORD deserves to be praised*. Show her respect — *praise her in public for what she has done* [emphasis added]. (Proverbs 31:30-31 CEV.)

She deserves praise! (And if you're saying to yourself that your wife does not honor the LORD, maybe if you start praising her, she will!) Proverbs 31 is one of the scripture passages that we refer to for a description of what most view as the quintessential Christian wife. Could it be that this woman described is so great (at least in part) because of how her husband speaks of her? Words are seeds. If you plant seeds of true praise, you are bound to have a flourishing wife.

Song of Solomon 4:16 (AMP) describes the wife as a garden:

> [You have called me a garden, she said] Oh, I pray that the [cold] north wind and the [soft] south wind may blow upon my garden, that its spices may flow out [in abundance for you in whom my soul delights]. *Let my beloved come into his garden and eat its choicest fruits* [emphasis added].

The wife is a garden, and the husband gets to enjoy the best of the fruit she produces. The one who expects to enjoy the best fruit of his garden should also be the one who cultivates and tends his garden with the utmost care. Words of praise and encouragement from her husband make the soil of the wife's spirit, soul and body rich.

According to Proverbs 18:21, "The tongue has the power of life and death, and those who love it will eat its fruit." The husband will eat the fruit of the words he speaks in his own life and he will eat the fruit of the words he speaks in his wife's life. With his words, the husband should speak life — praise and encouragement — to his wife. Even a natural plant will respond to words of praise and encouragement. How much more will the garden of your wife respond to the loving praise and encouragement of her beloved husband? What you want to grow, you must plant with your words. What you don't want to grow you must weed out with your words. Your words are the seed that will determine in large part what kind of fruit your wife will produce for you: whether it be bitter fruit or whether it be sweet.

Sow no seeds of insecurity. There's nothing at all wrong with a man respectfully admiring the virtues of other women, but there should be a distinction between how he looks at other women and how he looks at his wife. There should be a distinction between how he treats other women and how he treats his wife. There should be a distinction between how he speaks of other women, and how he speaks of his wife. Certain looks, actions and words of the husband should be reserved only for his wife. She should be the recipient of the best he has to offer. There is something wrong when a husband is full of praise for others but does not praise his own wife. As the saying goes, "It's a poor frog that doesn't praise

How Does Your Garden Grow?

his own pond!"

> Her children rise up and call her blessed (happy, fortunate, and to be envied); and *her husband boasts of and praises her, [saying]*, *Many daughters have done virtuously, nobly, and well [with the strength of character that is steadfast in goodness], but you excel them all* [emphasis added]. (Proverbs 31:28-29 AMP)

The husband of this woman is not denying the virtues of other women. He is celebrating them also. But, he makes it known to his wife that no matter what other women have going for them, none of them can hold a candle to her. Now, tell me, what wife would not respond positively to that kind of praise? Most women will not mind their husbands respectfully admiring other women if they know that their husbands admire them above all other women. But, if a wife is not admired by her husband, (or if she does not know that she is admired by him because he has not articulated or demonstrated that admiration to her), she may become insecure and jealous of others to whom her husband's admiration is notably given.

Carefully guard your marriage. Be jealous over your marriage by carefully tending your wife's garden, guarding and protecting it. With your words, put to death every weed, thorn and thistle that threatens the fruitfulness and health of your wife's garden. This applies also to bad word seed that others will try to plant in your wife's garden and in your marriage overall. Sometimes, there are those who are or will be jealous of your wife or jealous of your marriage and will attempt to sabotage it by planting negative word seeds. Don't allow it! As soon as you know that bad seed has fallen, root it out immediately! Confront the saboteur if necessary and reestablish the position and priority of your wife and your marriage. Root out anyone and everyone who seeks to tamper with the fruitfulness of your wife's garden. Better yet, be preemptive and before it has a chance to happen, let others know that your wife is *your* garden and you will not allow *anyone* to plant any bad seeds there. To those gentlemen who are engaged to be married, begin to prepare your male and female friends now for the primary position your wife to be will and must have in your life.

Walk in love. 1 Corinthians 13:4 tells us "love never is envious nor boils over with jealousy." This is not referring to your natural love, but to the love of God that the Holy Spirit has poured out in your heart (see Romans 5:5). This same love that God has put in your heart is the love wherewith you must love your wife. You must let what God has placed inside of your heart dominate your soul (i.e. your mind, will and emotions) and your flesh (i.e. your outward actions). This is what walking in love is all about. It's not based on your feelings but on what God has already enabled you to do.

As was said before, there is nothing wrong with wanting good things to happen in your own life. However, when you are unable to celebrate good things happening in the life of your wife, and feel that you should have what she has, you will find yourself in the clutches of ungodly jealousy. You do not need what she has: you need only what God has for you. Ungodly jealousy in the life of a believer is what happens when you are deceived into thinking that God has denied you something that is good that you believe you have a right to have. God went through a lot of trouble to make you completely unique. There is no one else on this earth who is exactly like you. God has a plan and purpose that is custom-made for you. No one else can carry out the purpose and plan God has for you. You are unique.

The way you will overcome ungodly jealousy is to know that God has a specific plan for your life and to know that He will not withhold any good thing from those who walk uprightly (Psalm 84:11). So, when you look at the blessings of others — including your wife — remind yourself that if you don't have what they have, it's either not good for you, or it's not good for you yet. God has not forgotten you.

A Word To The Wives

You are indeed blessed and highly favored, and to whom much is given much is also required. Remember that you also must walk in love. The same scripture that tells us that love never is envious nor boils over with jealousy, also tells us:

> [Love] is not boastful or vainglorious, does not display itself haughtily. It is not conceited (arrogant and inflated with pride); it is not rude (unmannerly) and does not act unbecomingly. (1 Corinthians 13:4b-5 AMP)

Be careful not to add fuel to the fire of ungodly jealousy by becoming boastful because of your God-given favor. By all means, shine. That is what God requires of you so that others can see your good works and glorify Him (see Matthew 5:16). And as you shine, encourage. When God brings you into the presence of great men and women, as opportunity is given, give honor to your husband. Speak well of him in their presence. As your ministry takes off, acknowledge your husband's covering. Even if he's functioning only as a figurehead right now, he's still your God-ordained head. Be careful to let the light of your favor encompass your husband, not eclipse him.

Pray that your husband will speak words that build you and your family and reflect a heart of love (see Proverbs 18:21; Ephesians 4:15, 29). Pray that your husband will discover and live his God-given purpose (see Jeremiah 29:11).

4

YOURS, MINE AND IRS

And the Lord God took the man and put him in the Garden of Eden to tend and guard and keep it. And the man and his wife were both naked and were not embarrassed or ashamed in each other's presence. (Genesis 2:15, 25 AMP)

Openness in marriage is an absolute necessity, especially when it comes to the area of finances. The financial status of your spouse (or spouse-to-be) should not come as a surprise. It should be openly and honestly discussed. It is said that finances is one of, if not *the* leading contributing factors to marriages ending in divorce. Some enter into marriage with the misconception that because "the two shall become one" there will be unity in their finances. Sometimes there is unity in the finances, but many times that's not the case. Even when there is not unity in the marriage, the financial affairs of the husband and wife will often be treated as one. For example, if one person in the marriage has great credit, and the other does not, both will be affected by the bad credit if they attempt to purchase or finance anything jointly. There are too many different financial issues for me to address them all here, but there is one issue in particular that I'd like to discuss.

Cheer Up Your Wife

One of the biggest financially related problems I've observed in Christian marriages is one that has more to do with order than with the finances themselves. When a woman marries she takes on her husband's name. The state of her name will not affect his name. However, the state of his name will affect hers. If a husband does not manage his financial affairs well, he will leave his wife bereft of financial security and a good name. One of the worst things a husband can do is to be a discredit to his wife financially. Bad credit; unwise financial decisions; lack of income; poor management or planning are all precursors to a bad name. When a wife takes on her husband's name it should not be a discredit to her but an asset. When that is not the case, there will be trouble in paradise.

The Bible says, "A good name is rather to be chosen than great riches..." (Proverbs 22:1). This is the value God places on having a good name. Lack of financial responsibility and integrity will give any man a bad name, and if he's married, his wife will also bear that bad name. Just ask the Internal Revenue Service (IRS). Even if the wife has all of her financial ducks in a row, if the husband is not doing what he needs to do as head of household (which is what he is supposed to be), the IRS will come after any assets she has as well. In God's "internal revenue service," He holds the man responsible for the welfare of His wife. Just ask Adam.

When the serpent deceived Eve, God didn't come to her asking any questions. He went directly to Adam and held him fully responsible for what happened to Eve. She talked to the serpent; she ate the forbidden fruit; she offered the fruit to her husband but God held *him* responsible. If this is God's mindset towards the responsibility of the husband with regards to the welfare of his wife, it should be our mindset also.

There has been a fraud perpetuated in Christian marriages particularly that says the wife should also function as financial provider for the marriage. This is out of order. I've witnessed wives getting burned out in their marriages because they've taken on the financial responsibilities of the household. It didn't matter if the wife was financially capable of taking on those responsibilities or if she was barely scraping by, the results were the same: utter and complete frustration. The only difference may have been that the wife who had very little financial resources to begin with might reach the burn out point faster than the wife who had ample resources. You would think that if a wife was financially capable of taking on the financial burdens of the household there wouldn't be a problem but that's not the case. As was said before, how finances are handled within marriage has more to do with order than with the actual finances; and when things are out of order, chaos within the marriage results.

When we look back in Genesis at God's original (and ideal) model for marriage, man is established in his relationship with his Creator, given purpose, given a job to do, and then given a wife. The wife comes into and under the provision of her husband that is already in place. She is not asked, commanded or instructed to help him work. She is set in place to help him as *he* works. I am well aware that we live in a world of liberated and independent women who may, at first glance, take offense to the point being made here but please bear with me; I'm not finished.

Cheer Up Your Wife

Am I suggesting that a woman not work? No, I am not. I am, however, stating that a woman who is married and has come under the provision and responsibility of her husband should not be asked, commanded or instructed to take on the role of financial provider in the marriage. If she works, it should be a *want* to not a *have* to, and any funds she has or makes should not be depended on for the financial upkeep of the marriage or household. It is the husband's duty and responsibility to work and be the financial provider for his household. I say this with the assumption that the husband is well, fit and able to work being fully aware that there are sometimes exceptional circumstances. But what is being dealt with here is the standard as God gave it and not the exception.

Show me a wife who has taken on the financial responsibilities of the marriage to the neglect of home and family and I will show you a frustrated, unhappy wife and an emasculated husband. That combination equals trouble every time. God's order is that the wife helps her husband as he works.

What's A Husband To Do?

When God came looking for Adam, He said "Where are you?" This is the question every "Adam" must ask and answer for himself: "Where am I spiritually? Where am I financially? Where am I with regards to the welfare of my wife?" Honestly ask yourself whether or not you have asked, implied, commanded or instructed your wife to take on any of the financial responsibilities of the household. If so, you are out of order (and if she has taken them on, so is she but we will address that later). Where there is disorder there is chaos. Where there is chaos there is confusion. Where there is confusion God is not. If your income is not enough to

Yours, Mine and IRS

adequately take care of your household, don't force or pressure your wife into getting a job. Instead, you get another one. Do what you need to do to cover the financial needs of your house legally and responsibly. It may require that you swallow your pride and take on a position for which you might otherwise feel you are over-qualified, but you must do what you must — within legal and moral limits — to take care of your household.

I remember some years back there was a mail man with whom I had become acquainted. When he would drop off the mail we would sometimes engage in conversation, and through our conversations I learned when he got married. After he got married, not only did he work overtime when he could to supplement his income, he also took on another part-time job so he could take care of the financial needs of his newly expanded household. His second job was at a grocery store stocking shelves and bagging groceries. When he told me this, my respect for him went through the roof! Some men would have thought it beneath them to have a "respectable" day job and then go and bag groceries at night, but this man had the right idea. He did what he needed to do not only so he could meet the financial needs of his household, but so that they could have the luxury of doing some things they didn't necessarily need but desired as well. They bought a new home, traveled and did other things they might not have been able to do had he not supplemented his income.

Years ago, a male mentor of mine gave me some great insight. He said, "A man will only be as much of a gentleman as you require him to be." While I would not apply this generally to all men, I have found this to be true of some. There are some men who are comfortable sitting back and letting their wives take on their responsibilities. They're okay with her being the breadwinner and taking care of all the financial business (especially if no one knows she's the one who's doing it). There are some men who, for whatever reason, are satisfied with doing only the bare minimum of what's expected of them. They are perfectly comfortable with their wives paying all the bills and taking care of every other financially related responsibility or handling the bulk of it, but that is out of order. Even if she wants to do it to help you out, don't allow her to take on the financial burden. Don't forbid her from working if that's what she really wants to do. If you are opposed to her working, pray individually and together for balance and a desire to carry out and function in God's order. If she does decide to work, make it clear that it's your God-given responsibility to take care of her and that her financial resources will be primarily for her wants not for "our" needs.

I have said for many years that you should be able to do more married than not. Otherwise, what's the point of getting married? There should be improvement, enhancement and progress. It is the man who is told to work and take care of the garden (see Genesis 2:15). He is to be the provider. That is God's order. The husband represents Christ and it is Christ who provides for His bride and not vice versa. If a wife chooses to work it should be optional not required and if the wife chooses to work, it should not be to alleviate the financial burden of the family. I know this may be an unpopular position, but God's ways have never been popular.

If you have managed your finances poorly in the past and

ruined your credit (or your wife's credit), make it your goal to restore your (and her) good name. Take the steps necessary — no matter how long it takes — to repair your credit so that when you need to move forward together, you taking the lead as the head of the household, it is not a hindrance. Put things in order financially so that if anything happens to you your wife is not left bearing the weight of your financial burdens.

Discuss with your wife what the financial strategy of your household should be. What works in your household may work a little differently in someone else's household. Find out what works for you. For example, sit down and discuss with your wife who is best suited to handle taking care of the administration of payments for the bills, etc. It may be that your wife is more administratively inclined than you are and is better equipped to make sure the bills are paid on time each time. If so, allow her to do what she is better suited to do. You may want to have a joint checking account that can be used for the finances you bring into the household (making sure she has access to the checks). Be transparent with her about everything concerning your financial affairs.

Here's another important point: as you establish (or reestablish, as the case may be) yourself as the financial provider, do not make her feel like a dependent child. She should not have to ask you for money. She should be able to freely access the resources you provide to take care of what she needs to take care of without having to ask your permission or give an accounting to you. If your wife needs to go to the store to purchase personal items, you should not need to know about it. You should not be checking her receipts or price tags. When God put Adam and Eve in the Garden of Eden He also put the tree of life there and told them you can freely eat of it. Even though Adam was the primary caretaker of the Garden, Eve did not need permission to take what she needed or wanted. Everything that was provided for him before she got there became just as much hers to freely access and use as it was his.

Do your utmost best to see to it that your wife looks her best. You should not be looking like you just walked out of a *GQ Magazine* advertisement while your wife can't even buy an outfit for herself. She should not be driving around in an unreliable, mechanically malfunctioning rust bucket while you ride around in the latest model car. If anything, put her in the latest model and you drive the rust bucket until you can do better. You will be the hero as you imitate Christ giving His best for His bride. As your wife, she has come under your (lowercase) lordship which implies that you have now taken responsibility not just for her needs but for her (reasonable) wants also.

A wise woman knows how to "make a silk purse out of a sow's ear." She'll get the best quality for the best price; she'll make even a little go a long way; and she'll see to it that her family is taken care of as well. If your wife is not functioning in wisdom in how she manages/uses money, as her head and leader, pray with her and for her that wisdom is granted her to function according to godly financial principles, and you model the same.

Always remember that when a man takes a wife, it's his responsibility to take care of her and not vice versa. All things being equal, assuming the man is in good health and of sound mental capacity, he should work. The wife working under such circumstances should be optional not required. In the beginning when God made man, He made sure man had a job to do before a wife was introduced into the picture. When God was ready to present Eve to Adam, He said He would provide him with a suitable helper which at its simplest level suggests that the man was doing something already because a person doesn't need help to do nothing. God adds to make better and to enhance not to replace what He has already established. When the wife is placed in the position of "helping" with the finances, it takes the responsibility that should rest on the husband's shoulders and puts it on hers. God has equipped the man for it. The financial provision of the home and family should not be predicated upon what the wife does or doesn't do. The husband is to provide for the wife and for the family. God will bless and help the man who desires and makes every effort to function under God's order.

A Word To The Wives

It is the nature of a godly wife to want to help her husband, and this is good. It is part of her role and function in the marriage. However, the problem a lot of wives have is they help too much! She often takes on what she is not supposed to take on. In her willingness to make things easier for her husband, she makes things tougher on herself and many times, eventually winds up resenting him for the burden she now feels she has to carry. She helps so much that she ends up taking over and taking on so much of the husband's responsibilities that it overwhelms her.

Wife, you will have to take a step of faith: step back! Take a step back and allow your husband to step up. Give him the opportunity to be the provider. Pray for him and express your confidence in God's ability to provide for you through your husband. It is in the nature of a man to rise to a challenge but if you step in and take on every challenge for him, what's a husband to do? Every godly husband wants to be his wife's hero. Give him room to step into his role and to take on the responsibilities that God has equipped him to handle. He may resist initially because complacency or even fear may have set in. He may even struggle at first, but resist the urge to "rescue" him. Allow the man in him, the leader in him, the husband in him to rise up.

True love, God's love, does what's in the best interest of the other person. Be a virtuous excellent wife. The woman spoken of in Proverbs 31 had the liberty to buy and sell as she pleased and she also saw to it that her husband was respected and her household was well cared for. Make it your goal to live out Proverbs 31:11-12 (NIV) which says:

> Her husband has full confidence in her and lacks nothing of value. She brings him good, not harm, all the days of her life.

As your husband makes all his resources available to you, make sure that he is well taken care of. When the Lord turns his heart and he steps into his role as financial provider, don't abuse your privileges. Manage the affairs of your household well.

While God realigns your husband to take his role and full responsibility as financial provider, make Hebrews 13:5-6 (AMP)

Yours, Mine and IRS

your daily confession:

> Let your character or moral disposition be free from love of money [including greed, avarice, lust, and craving for earthly possessions] and be satisfied with your present [circumstances and with what you have]; for He [God] Himself has said, I will not in any way fail you nor give you up nor leave you without support. [I will] not, [I will] not, [I will] not in any degree leave you helpless nor forsake nor let [you] down (relax My hold on you)! [Assuredly not!] So we take comfort and are encouraged and confidently and boldly say, The Lord is my Helper; I will not be seized with alarm [I will not fear or dread or be terrified]. What can man do to me?

5

BABY MAMA DRAMA

Two are better than one, because they have a good [more satisfying] reward for their labor. (Ecclesiastes 4:9 AMP)

Children are an investment in marriage. The way children are treated is determined by how valuable an asset they are deemed to be. I have often heard children being described more as a liability than an asset: viewed more as something that detracts from the marriage rather than something that adds to it. This kind of perspective will undoubtedly adversely affect the marriage relationship.

When my second child was born, my firstborn was excited about the birth of his little sister and he couldn't wait for her to come home from the hospital. He had spent months beforehand imagining how they would play together and have all kinds of fun and good times. But when she did come home, the reality of having a newborn in the house set in. She seemingly got all the attention, and after so many years of enjoying the undivided attention of being an only child, having to share the time and attention to which he had become accustomed with someone else was a difficult adjustment for him to make.

Cheer Up Your Wife

In a similar manner, when a new baby comes into a marriage a husband may find himself struggling with the reality of no longer being the center of attention in his wife's heretofore childless world. Before the children, he may have been the focus of all her attention. But, after the baby is born she now has another love in her life; another person she adores; someone else she's completely devoted to; someone who's every little movement and accomplishment brings her great delight and evokes from her the most lavish praise. Sometimes, without even fully realizing it, the husband begins to feel replaced, and though few may admit it, he may even find himself jealous of his own child.

Children do place a demand on every marriage, but it was not intended for one person to solely meet that demand. God's strategy is that the needs of the child be met by both mother and father. Children require spiritual guidance, emotional and financial support, physical affection, discipline and lots of love and attention to name a few. All of these needs ideally should be met by both mother and father. A man is not designed to be a mother, and a woman is not designed to be a father; the child needs both. However, the sad reality is that in some marriages, even between a believing wife and a believing husband, the wife finds herself feeling and functioning like a single parent because of the physical, emotional, spiritual and/or financial absence of the husband. A husband can be physically present in the home but otherwise absent leaving the child's demands for love, guidance, support and affection solely on the mother. This places undue strain and stress on the wife which consequently translates to conflict in the marriage.

Baby Mama Drama

A husband's expression of love for his wife's child is an expression of love for her. If a husband is kind towards his wife's children, she will experience that kindness to a degree that is just as, if not more intense than if it were shown towards her directly. This is why one of the most romantic and loving things a husband can do for his wife is to show love and kindness to her child, especially if he does so consistently.

Conversely, a husband can wound his wife and kill her respect for him through her womb. What I mean by this is that the way a husband treats his wife's children, whether they are his by blood or by marriage, affects her emotionally and also affects her perception of him. There is nothing more hurtful to a mother than seeing her child wounded or in any kind of pain, especially if that pain is caused by someone else she loves, in this case, her husband.

Most mothers see their children as a more sensitive and vulnerable extension of themselves. That child came from her womb, and even if the child is not hers by birth, the connection to her heart is just as real. If you mistreat the fruit of the tree, what are you saying about the tree from which they came? They are connected. Treat the fruit with care and you will honor the tree that bore it.

If you are a husband who is doing your best to treat your wife with love, honor and kindness and she still seems less than cheerful, it may not be the way you are treating her directly that is the problem: it may be the way you are interacting (or not interacting as the case may be) with your children.

Cheer Up Your Wife

Every husband should realize his importance and uniqueness as a father. A husband simply cannot be replaced by a child. God has uniquely equipped and ordained you to represent Him not just as a husband but as a father. What an honor! When you carry out your God-given responsibilities as a husband and a father, you will automatically alleviate any burden your wife may be carrying in that regard.

How you treat your children is a reflection of the honor you show for your wife.

> In the same way you married men should live considerately with [your wives], with an intelligent recognition [of the marriage relation], *honoring the woman as [physically] the weaker* [emphasis added], but [realizing that you] are joint heirs of the grace (God's unmerited favor) of life, in order that your prayers may not be hindered and cut off. [Otherwise you cannot pray effectively.] (1 Peter 3:7, AMP)

The woman is described as the "weaker" vessel in that she is not divinely designed to carry certain loads by herself or at all. Not that she is not capable: she is not designed for it, and there is a difference between capability and design.

A chair is designed for sitting, though most are capable of being stood upon. It is designed to carry weight, but that weight is supposed to be distributed in a certain way. If you put too much weight on one particular area of the chair, you risk damage to the structure and balance of the design as it was intended. Some products have a weight capacity that indicates the maximum load that can be supported. Each woman has an innate God-given weight capacity. As long as she has not exceeded her maximum capacity, and as long as the weight is distributed where it needs to be, she will be able to bear the load. But if the weight capacity is exceeded, although it may seem she is able to support it, it's only a matter of time before she gives way – emotionally, mentally, physically or even spiritually – under that weight.

Every day we see women who take on roles and responsibilities of men/husbands that, although they seem capable of carrying out, they are not designed to bear. Whenever a woman takes on what she is not designed to carry, things are out of order, and when things are out of order, chaos is guaranteed to show up somewhere: mentally, physically, emotionally, and/or spiritually.

What's A Husband To Do?

The Bible encourages us to bear each other's burdens and in so doing, fulfill the law of Christ (see Galatians 6:2). The law of Christ is a law of love. Husband, love your wife enough to alleviate the burden of her having to feel and function like a single parent.

A big source of contention in marriage can be caused by how the husband perceives his role in relation to his child and how he perceives his wife's role in relation to his child. So much so that if the husband does not realize and value his own unique and special connection to the child, he could find himself feeling as if he is competing with his own child. This can easily happen if the husband compares how his wife treats the child to how she treats him as a husband. That, however, is like comparing an apple to an orange: they are two different kinds of relationships, each cultivated differently.

For example, if the husband feels the wife is more affectionate towards the child than she is towards him, instead of focusing on why she expresses more affection to the child, time needs to be taken to discover what hinders her from expressing herself affectionately towards him (her husband). God has given each of us an infinite capacity to love, and that love is not mutually exclusive. Just because your wife loves her child doesn't mean she loves you any less and just because your wife loves you doesn't mean she loves her child any less; differently, but not less. If she is expressing affection to the child, she is obviously capable of expressing affection. So her ability to express affection would not be the issue. Perhaps there may be a root of bitterness that has developed in her because of her husband's lack of involvement with the child. Get to the root of what you see as a problem. This may require you to be vulnerable in expressing the way you feel, but it can also provide your wife with the opportunity to reassure, reaffirm and/or reemphasize your unique place as husband and father. Take the time to find out from her where she sees room for improvement. Try not to interpret her feedback as just negative criticism but as incentive for how you can improve your relationship with her by supporting the burden that you are designed to carry as a father.

Women are sometimes made to feel like they have to choose between their relationship with their husbands and their relationship with their children. This should not even be an issue. Each relationship is ordained by God and each relationship has it's place and priority. As a considerate and mature husband, recognize that there will be times when circumstances will require that your wife give more attention to the child than you. Conversely, there are times when you will be required to give more attention to your child than to your wife. To do one does not diminish the importance of the other. If a wife is forced to choose — and she should never have to feel like she has to — between the needs of her child, especially a young child, and the wants of her husband, she may choose the child, not because she does not want to fulfill the desires of her husband, but because she is divinely wired to give attention to the child who she views as more helpless or vulnerable. Instead of putting your wife in a position where she feels she has to choose between your wants and the child's needs, support her in meeting the needs of the child and then you will free her up to cater to your wants.

I have been known to say that marriage is a mirror: it will reflect the true image of who you are both to yourself and to your spouse. Sometimes you'll like what you see and sometimes you won't, but that doesn't make the reflection any less of a reality. I later discovered that when you have children, it's like going into a dressing room that is surrounded with mirrors. You are reflected and scrutinized from every possible angle. Not only can the children see the true you reflected, your spouse also sees and takes note of not just you but the image of the reflection your child sees. Don't get mad at the mirror for showing you what's there. If you don't like the reflection you see, take whatever steps necessary and feasible to change it.

Imitate your Father.

Cheer Up Your Wife

> THEREFORE BE imitators of God [copy Him and follow His example], as well-beloved children [imitate their father].
>
> Watch what God does, and then you do it, like children who learn proper behavior from their parents. (Ephesians 5:1 AMP and MSG)

You may not have had your earthly father in your life to show you how to be a good father, but you have a heavenly Father who is a wonderful example. If you want to know how to be a good father, look at what God does and follow His example. Here are a few ways you can imitate God as a father.

Tell your children how much you love them and how proud you are of them... even (and especially) before they've done anything loving or praiseworthy.

> And lo a voice from heaven, saying, "This is my beloved Son, in whom I am well pleased." (Matthew 3:17 KJV)

God called David a man after His own heart (see Acts 13:22) knowing that David would make grievous mistakes. God expressed love and approval of His Son before Jesus did anything in ministry. God also encourages us by calling us loved, righteous, worthy and a whole host of other encouraging things long before we realize them. His words encourage and empower us to live up to who He says we are. Encourage your child when he/she does something good, but don't wait until they've done something good to encourage them. Encourage them before they've done anything good and they may be more apt to do good. When they've done wrong, instruct and discipline them as necessary, and find a way to encourage them to do better. Discipline without encouragement is a poor motivator. When you encourage your child, you encourage your wife.

Give your child affection and attention.

> So he got up and came to his [own] father. But while he was still a long way off, his father saw him and was moved with pity and tenderness [for him]; and he ran and embraced him and kissed him [fervently]. (Luke 15:20 AMP)

You may not be comfortable showing a lot of affection towards your child, but start somewhere. Try starting with a smile. When was the last time you just looked into the face of your son or daughter and just smiled at him/her? A smile is an expression of affection and your smile in particular communicates volumes to your child. It says, "I approve of you. You're beautiful in my eyes. I love you. I am pleased with you." Smile at your child. One smile from Dad will brighten your child's day and cheer your wife's heart.

Tell your child that you love him/her and show affection. Some men find it easier to be affectionate towards their daughters, but sons also need to be embraced; sons need to be kissed by their fathers; sons need to be touched by their fathers in loving and affirming ways also. As Dr. Mike Murdock said, "The absence of a father empowers those who are present." If you don't show your children appropriate affection, you will make them vulnerable to other men who may show them inappropriate affection.

Cheer Up Your Wife

Don't show more affection or attention to other children than you do to your own. If you do, you may foster feelings of rejection and discouragement in your own children. Make sure you honor *your* children. All children are special, but your own children should be most special to you, and they should feel that they are most special to you. Borrowing another quote from Dr. Mike Murdock, "If you treat everybody the same, you honor no one." Honoring your child is honoring your wife.

Bless your children.

> Blessed be the God and Father of our Lord Jesus Christ, who hath blessed us... (Ephesians 1:3 KJV)

One of the most unexpected and life-impacting moments for me was when my father blessed me. It was really informal and I was an adult at the time, but I distinctly remember feeling as if that blessing was something I had been longing for and hadn't even realized it. God "calls those things which do not exist as though they did" (Romans 4:17), and you can do the same. Speak good things over the lives of your children, and speak good things to them about their lives. The Lord will use your words to bring your children into alignment with His plans and purpose for their lives.

Teach your children the word and ways of God.

> Love God, your God, with your whole heart: love him with all that's in you, love him with all you've got! Write these commandments that I've given you today on your hearts. Get them inside of you and then get them inside your children. Talk about them

> wherever you are, sitting at home or walking in the street; talk about them from the time you get up in the morning to when you fall into bed at night. (Deuteronomy 6:5-7 MSG)

As a father, you are your child's role model and you are one of the greatest influences in your child's life. Don't set a hypocritical standard by requiring of them what you yourself are unwilling to do. Teach them by example how to love and serve God with everything they've got. You may not be a preacher or a Bible scholar, but you can still see to it that they learn the Word of God. Even if you feel you can't teach it, expose them to others who can, and share with them what you have learned from it. You will be the best Bible your child will ever read.

Discipline your children.

> For the Lord corrects and disciplines everyone whom He loves... For what son is there whom his father does not [thus] train and correct and discipline? (Hebrews 12:6-7 AMP)

> Fathers, do not irritate and provoke your children to anger [do not exasperate them to resentment], but rear them [tenderly] in the training and discipline and the counsel and admonition of the Lord. (Ephesians 6:4 AMP)

Appropriate and well-timed discipline is an act of love. The father is the first representation of God a child sees. How you treat your child as a father greatly impacts how that child expects God to treat him/her. If you are critical of and judgmental towards your child, that child is likely to perceive God as being critical and judgmental. If you are a harsh disciplinarian, your child is likely to be fearful of God expecting him to punish his/her every wrong move. If you are loving and affectionate, and take the time to give instruction along with the discipline, it will make it easier for a child to accept God the Father as loving and affectionate and to accept and follow His instruction.

Be an example (to your son) of how a husband is to love his wife, and be an example (to your daughter) of how a wife is to be loved by her husband.

> Husbands, go all out in your love for your wives, exactly as Christ did for the church—a love marked by giving, not getting. Christ's love makes the church whole. His words evoke her beauty. *Everything he does and says is designed to bring the best out of her, dressing her in dazzling white silk, radiant with holiness. And that is how husbands ought to love their wives. They're really doing themselves a favor—since they're already "one" in marriage.*
> No one abuses his own body, does he? No, he feeds and pampers it. That's how Christ treats us, the church, since we are part of his body. And this is why a man leaves father and mother and cherishes his wife. No longer two, they become "one flesh." This is a huge mystery, and I don't pretend to understand it all. What is clearest to me is the way Christ treats the church. And this provides a good picture of how each husband is to treat his wife, *loving himself in loving her...* [emphasis added] (Ephesians 5:25-33 MSG)

Baby Mama Drama

Fathers are the glory of their children (see Proverbs 17:6) and the Bible teaches that the woman is the glory of the man (see 1 Corinthians 11:7). You show your child what glory is supposed to look like as a father and what glory is supposed to look like on a husband. You are the first representation of a husband your child will see. You will, through your actions, teach your son how to treat his wife, and teach your daughter how she can expect to be treated. Of course, as your child matures he/she will ultimately make his/her own decisions, but that does not change the fact that you, as the father, are the first representation of what a husband is like.

It is extremely important that you do your best to represent God accurately. Moses was not allowed to enter the promised land not just because he struck the rock instead of speaking to it, but because in striking the rock, he misrepresented who God was to His people (see Numbers 20:12). God does not like to be misrepresented. Remember that as you represent Him as father and husband. Be careful that you don't cause your child to believe something about God that is not true.

Treat your children as holy.

> For the Christian wife brings holiness to her marriage, and the Christian husband brings holiness to his marriage. Otherwise, your children would not be holy, but now they are holy. (1 Corinthians 7:14 NLT)

The Bible says that you as a believer bring holiness to your marriage. The same is true of the believing wife. As a result, your children are holy. Handle, treat, speak to your children in a manner that is befitting who God says they are: holy.

You are representing God the Father. What an honor with which the Father has entrusted you! No other family member carries this distinction. You have the greater honor and consequently, you have the greater responsibility. Remember that your child is an investment in your marriage – a most valuable asset – and your child is an extension of the heart of your wife.

A Word To The Wives

Under normal circumstances, most women are nurturers and instinctive caregivers, and that's a wonderful thing. But, no matter how good a mother you are, you are not built to do it all, all the time. As much as possible, allow your child's father to carry out his responsibilities as a father, even if that means at times stepping back to allow him to do it. Your husband may not do everything just the way you might do it, but as long as he is not doing anything to harm or injure the child, let him do his part.

Don't allow pride, anger or bitterness to keep you from getting the help you need. If you need help, ask for it. If you feel overloaded, tell him. If your husband is dealing with your child in a way that hurts your heart, express it. Don't take on your husband's responsibilities when he is right there and able to carry them out himself. Make sure that when God examines the order of the marriage and the husband's responsibilities as a father, He does not have to ask you to step aside in order to see what your husband is doing.

6

PILLOW TALK

The husband should fulfill his wife's sexual needs...

The husband should give to his wife her conjugal rights (goodwill, kindness, and what is due her as his wife)... (1 Corinthians 7:3 NLT and AMP)

Presumption is the enemy of true sexual intimacy. I believe if you would poll married men who are actively and consistently engaging their wives sexually, most, if not all, of them would believe they were satisfying their wives. But, I also believe if you polled those same wives, their answers might differ from their husbands.

When a man comes into a marriage with prior sexual experience he may make the mistake of believing that he already knows how to satisfy his wife sexually. That would be a mistake. While it may have been true, at least in his mind, that he satisfied some other woman, the woman he married is not the same as an "other woman."

Every woman's body is unique. A man could touch his wife

Cheer Up Your Wife

where he touched another woman expecting or assuming he'd get the same reaction or level of arousal with his wife and get absolutely nothing. He may have blown in Suzy's ear and got her really excited, but when he blows in his wife Betty's ear it irritates her to no end. The sad part is unless he's really in tune with his wife's responses or reactions (or lack thereof), he may not even notice.

Just because a woman engages sexually does not mean she is satisfied at the conclusion. A wife can reach climax and still be left feeling unsatisfied. A wife wants to be pleasured on purpose. She doesn't want to be touched so she can be aroused just so her husband can get her to the place where she can be more readily penetrated. She wants to be touched knowing her husband enjoys touching her and because it brings her pleasure.

Each woman has parts of her body that are more sensitive to touch than others and that can stir intense levels of arousal. If her husband has not taken the time to explore what those areas are, he may never experience his wife's full potential as a lover. Granted, not every woman knows what those areas are, but a husband who is really concerned about pleasuring his wife should take the time to find out.

Touch is extremely important in the language of love. Time should be spent not just "going for the gold," so to speak, but carefully and intentionally excavating the surrounding areas to see what other treasures can be mined. A woman's body is constantly changing, so what worked for her six months ago may not work for her now. If she's had children, what worked for her pre-

Pillow Talk

pregnancy may be ineffective or very different now. That's good and exciting news for every husband because he has a lifelong opportunity to hunt for new treasure.

Something else to keep in mind is that there are different ways to express touch. You can't handle an egg the same way you handle a melon. In other words, you can't touch everything the same way. The touch of lips is different from the touch of fingertips. The feel of the skin on the palm of the hand is different from the feel of the skin on the back of the hand. The body responds differently to varying degrees of pressure and temperature, but all are communicated by touch.

Not only is touch extremely important to a woman, words are also. Men and women are both created in God's image: we each carry different characteristics of His personality. A man tends to want praise: he wants to hear words that applaud his *accomplishments* as a man. Whereas a woman desires worship: she wants to hear words that extol *who she is* as a woman. A woman can be as moved by words as she is by touch.

A lot is said across the pulpit about how a wife must see to it that she "renders due benevolence" (1 Corinthians 7:3 KJV) to her husband. This is often interpreted as, the wife should make sure her husband is satisfied sexually whenever he wants to be. Often this line of thinking is punctuated with warnings to the wife about how her husband may be lured away by another woman because of her (the wife's) unfulfilled sexual obligation. Interestingly enough, I have never heard a sermon about the converse scenario. I have never heard anyone talk about how a wife can also be tempted sexually due to her husband's unfulfilled sexual obligation. The truth of the matter is there are some wives who are actually more interested in sexual intimacy than their husbands.

I would venture to say that there are probably a lot more unfulfilled wives than husbands because for most women, sexual intercourse is not just about physical consummation. Women need to connect mentally and emotionally as well. If a wife has an unfulfilled emotional desire or a mental process that has not been brought to closure, she may find it difficult to connect with her husband on a physical level. Recognizing this is one way a husband can live with his wife in an understanding manner (see 1 Peter 3:7).

It's not enough, and it is emphatically wrong, for a husband to demand sex because it's the wife's biblical "duty." That would be an inappropriate application of scripture and grossly missing the point. The husband needs to see his wife as more than just a body that can be used to satisfy his physical needs. Furthermore, to try to enforce one scripture while ignoring or negating another is an imbalanced approach. The sexual act is supposed to be an act of love in marriage, and loving God's way is about willingness not force or "spiritually" punctuated emotional blackmail. Before a husband tries to use "render due benevolence" (1 Corinthians 7:3 KJV) to try to convince (or force) his wife to fulfill his sexual demands, he would be wise to also consider the following:

> Each of you should give as you have decided in your heart to give. You should not be sad when you give, and you should not give because you feel forced to give. God loves the person who gives happily. (2 Corinthians 9:7 NCV)

Pillow Talk

This scripture is in the context of giving, but don't miss the principle and/or limit it to only financial giving. God is concerned about the heart attitude in any kind of giving, and a wise and loving husband should share the same concern. If a husband finds that his wife is reluctant to give herself to him sexually, he would be wise to find out why. Perhaps the wife is tired, and if so, why is she so tired that she would not want to engage in what is normally a very pleasurable activity? Find out why and what can be done about it. Perhaps the wife is in physical pain. Maybe she really does have a headache. It could be that the wife is dealing with some emotional turmoil or mental distress. Not having sex is not the problem: it's a symptom of a deeper root cause.

Don't just get upset with your wife because she didn't have sex with you. According to 1 Peter 3:7 (AMP), it is a God-given mandate for a husband to be considerate of his wife which would necessitate him at least trying to get to the heart of the matter to find out why she is reluctant to engage sexually.

Another side of the coin is when the husband withholds sexual intimacy from his wife. When a husband does not engage with his wife sexually, or does not fulfill her pleasure when he does, she becomes more vulnerable to the possibility of engaging with someone who she thinks may be more willing or able to satisfy her sexually. That does not presuppose that she will necessarily act on the temptation. But whether she does or not, that protective barrier that should be enforced by the consideration of her own husband becomes vulnerable to attack. Remember, just as it is commonly said that what the wife won't do somebody else will, the same is true of the husband: what he is unwilling to do, somebody else will.

Cheer Up Your Wife

It would be foolish for a husband to assume that what he doesn't want no one else does.

What's A Husband To Do?

Get to know your wife. The Bible refers to sexual intimacy as *knowing* your wife. This goes beyond just the physical sexual act of knowing her. You should know her intimately. What does she like? How does she like it? How does she like to be touched? When does she like to be touched? Where does she like to be touched. This will require you to tune in to your wife's responses and reactions. Don't do just enough to get her to the place where you can be satisfied. Take the time to do what it takes to get her to the place where she can be satisfied. Don't presume to know what she likes or doesn't like. Take the time to find out who she is.

One of the ways God expresses His love for us is by paying attention to the details. The Bible tells us that He numbers the very hairs on our heads (see Matthew 10:30). Counting the hairs on our heads is indicative of careful and loving attention, but God takes it a step further. He goes beyond just knowing what's there (i.e. counting hairs) to intimate knowledge of each detail (i.e. numbering hairs). If you want to be a great lover, take a clue from The Greatest Lover. Be interested in and cherish even the most minute details about your wife. Study your wife and learn her. No one (on earth) should express more interest in your wife than you.

Worship your wife. Worship, in its most basic sense, means to ascribe worth. A wife who doesn't feel she is worth much to her husband can be lured away with words: words that she either does not hear or does not believe from her husband. Take a lesson from

Pillow Talk

a king lover in how to love a woman with words.

In Solomon's Song of Songs (see Song of Solomon, chapters 1 – 8, MSG), an intimate portrait of a bride and her king lover is given. The words are the words of a lover and her response to him. He speaks of her cheeks; the curve of her neck; her jewelry; her fragrance; her eyes, face and voice. He describes her beauty; her hair; her smile; her lips; the lines of her neck; her breasts; the curve of her body. He admires her beauty from head to toe. He speaks of how she has captured his heart; how one look from her makes him feel; how hopelessly in love with her he is. He speaks of how beautiful her love is to him; he compliments even the scent of her clothes. He speaks of how he loves her body and soul. He speaks of her as a beautiful garden full of delectable things for him alone to enjoy. He speaks of her feet, even the way they look in her shoes. He speaks of how she moves; her elegant limbs. He talks about the shape of her body; the look and feel of her skin. He talks about her profile and how he desires her when he looks at her. He speaks of her outside and inside beauty; he speaks of her height; the taste of her tongue and lips. He describes her as beyond comparison. There's not a woman on earth in her right mind that wouldn't want to be spoken to by her lover in this way. No woman in her right mind would hear words like this, believe them and not respond.

Don't allow anyone else to out-talk you. Look for things that are attractive about your wife — not necessarily what she does, but things about *her* — and take the time to tell her about them. If you're blessed with a wife others find attractive, don't let others express that to her more than you. No one else should express more desire and *worthship* for your wife than you. Give your wife the words she needs to affirm what she's worth to you. Tell her what you love about her. Tell her what you find attractive about her. Tell her how much you desire her. Tell her how she adds value to your life. Tell her in what ways she excels in your eyes above other women. Don't flatter her with empty words that sound good but don't mean anything to you (or her). Tell her what is good *and* true.

Reserve a place of honor with your eyes that is for your wife only. If you treat everything the same, nothing is special. If you look at other women the same way you look at your wife, or worse yet, if you look at other women in a way that expresses *more* interest in them than your own wife, you will rob her of the honor of intimacy with your eyes. Lot was a married and upright man yet he said he made a covenant with his eyes not to look lustfully at another woman:

> I made a solemn pact with myself never to undress a
> girl with my eyes. (Job 31:4 MSG)

There is nothing wrong with appreciating the attractiveness of another, but there are some things (looks, words, gestures) that should be reserved for your wife alone. Honor your wife with your eyes and the rest will follow.

Appreciate who she is at every stage of life. Every season of life brings it's own blessings. Whether your wife is in the spring, summer, fall or winter of her life, look for and appreciate the blessings and bounty of each season. Women are naturally body-conscious. As a woman ages, as she has children, as life in general takes it's toll, especially if she is or has been an unhappy wife — all these things affect a woman's body. Every wife wants to be loved unconditionally. She wants to know that whether her body looks like a Coca Cola® bottle or a quart box, she is accepted by you and attractive to you at every stage and phase of life. If she does not feel you love her body, she will be reluctant to love you with it.

Love the one you're with. Your wife should not have to dress up like another woman in order to satisfy you sexually. Neither should she have to watch another woman (or man) having sex in order for you to be aroused. Learn how to be satisfied with what you have (see Philippians 4:12). Don't expect your wife to act out your past sexual escapades or fantasies. Stay in the moment; stay focused and stay faithful in your mind.

Invest in your wife's rest. Many wives do not get much opportunity to really rest. The less rest they get, the more irritable, unproductive and frustrated they may become. Encourage your wife to nourish her spirit, soul and body with rest. Send her on getaways. Treat her to a day at the spa. Let her sleep in late. Encourage her to go for a girls night out. Allow her time in each day to rest and relax. Allow her and even provide opportunities for her to rejuvenate. A rested wife is a calmer, more productive and happier person.

A Word To The Wives

Find ways to bring enjoyment and pleasure into your own life. Jesus came to give you life to the full (see John 10:10 AMP), so make a commitment to live your life to its maximum potential. Sexual intimacy should be a wonderful part of marriage, but it's just that: a *part*. Whether that part of your marriage is being fulfilled now or not, remember it's just a part. I have never heard of anyone dying because they were unfulfilled sexually.

Instead of bemoaning what you don't have, focus on what you do have. Instead of dwelling on what you can't do, focus on what you can do. Love yourself. Nourish yourself. Build yourself up. Become the healthiest, happiest you that you can be. When Jesus said He came to give you life more abundantly (John 10:10), He did not predicate the fullness of your life on anyone else's involvement but His own. In other words, it's not up to your husband to fulfill your life: it's up to *you*! Christ in *you* is the hope of glory (Colossians 1:27). Jesus has given you a V.I.P. pass to a fulfilled life. What you do with it is up to you.

God has designed the body to release "feel good" hormones called endorphins. Sex is one way to release endorphins but not the only way. When you smile (even if it's a fake smile) or laugh, endorphins are released. Other ways to release endorphins include exercising; eating something spicy; heightening your senses by experiencing something that moves you like a good movie or book; a work of art or beautiful scenery; something pleasant to the touch; or some inspiring music; eating a piece of dark chocolate; thinking positive thoughts. All these things release endorphins so don't limit your pleasure to just one thing. Fill your life with good and pleasurable things you enjoy and be the best most fulfilled you that you can be.

Tell yourself the good things you want to hear. Don't wait for your husband or anyone else to tell you that your beautiful and

Pillow Talk

attractive and loved. Look in the mirror and tell yourself. Smile at yourself. Appreciate yourself. Celebrate yourself! Learn to love yourself. Understand that The Greatest Lover in the universe wants you, even in your worst state. On good hair days and bad hair days, He loves you; light and lean, overflowing with abundance, and everything in between, He loves you; stretch marked or super toned, He loves you. No matter what state you find yourself in, *He loves you!*

APPENDIX 1

When A Husband Lies

I have spoken with many women who have been lied to in one form or another by their husbands. Ironically, in every instance the husband seemed clueless as to the effect of his lie on his wife and his marriage. To him, his lie was no big deal; but to her, that same lie left her feeling devastated and wondering whether or not she wanted to continue in the marriage. Is lying a big deal? Let's see.

The Lie

The most obvious meaning of a lie is something that is not true: a false statement deliberately presented as being true. But a lie is not so simplistic: it penetrates to a level deeper than simple falsehood. To lie is to breach the confidence and trust of another; it is an act of infidelity. A lie is intent to deceive; it is a treacherous act.

You can lie with your words and you can lie without speaking a word. When a husband leads his wife to believe that he is in one place and knows that he has made plans to be somewhere else and has not disclosed those plans to her, he has lied: he has intentionally deceived her. When a husband has taken on the responsibility of paying the bills and the wife later discovers that they are delinquent, he has lied: he has betrayed her trust. When a husband does not tell his wife the truth about this, that or the other (or him, her or whomever) because he "knows how she will react," he has lied: he has willfully withheld the truth.

Appendix 1

In scripture, very strong language is used to describe how God feels about lying: it is described as an abomination and detestable. What does that mean in plain language? It means that God hates lying; He regards it with horror; He finds it utterly and completely repulsive and disgusting. If God feels that way about lying, shouldn't we?

The Cause

Why did these husbands lie? In each instance there were three common denominators: fear, arrogance and selfishness. Fear says, I will lie because I'm afraid of the consequence of telling the truth. A lie is a cowardly way of dealing with (or not dealing with) an issue. Lying because you're afraid of a presumed consequence is foolish because the repercussion of a lie is worse than the consequence you thought you were avoiding. Arrogance says, I will lie because I should not have to deal with the consequence of telling the truth. When a husband lies to his wife he is in effect saying that she is not worthy of being told the truth. Selfishness says, I will lie because the consequence of telling the truth may get in the way of what I want to do. Lying to your wife is a blatant disregard of God's mandate to put the needs and interests of your wife above your own (see Philippians 2:3).

The Effect

When a husband lies to his wife he loses three things: trust, security and respect. Trust is built on truth. When a husband consistently does the good and right things that he says he will do, he will gain or regain his wife's trust. Speaking the truth is one of the most loving things we can do in marriage. When a husband lies,

When A Husband Lies

his word loses weight and the weight of a man's word anchors his integrity. When a husband lies, his wife is no longer sure that his yes means yes and his no means no. Now she questions what he says. His lie has sown seeds of doubt in the marriage and the fruit of doubt is distrust. God requires the wife to forgive her husband for lying to her, but God does not require her to trust him. Trust is earned, and it is earned by a commitment to being consistently truthful over time.

A husband is supposed to be the loving leader of his wife, but when a husband lies to his wife he is misleading her making it difficult for her to follow his leadership. She no longer feels safe because the one who has been set in place for her protection has caused her to feel vulnerable and made a fool of. The husband will reap the fear he has sown through the insecurity his lie has cultivated within his wife.

I believe that every husband wants to be his wife's hero. He wants to stand tall in her eyes; he wants her respect. But if through a lie he has shown her no consideration, it will be difficult for her to show him consideration. If through a lie he has not esteemed her, it will be difficult for her to esteem him. A lie is one of the most disrespectful things a husband can do to his wife, and as he robs her of respect by lying to her, he will rob himself of her respect.

The Conclusion

We do reap what we sow. When a husband lies he sows distrust, disrespect and insecurity into his marriage, and he will

Appendix 1

surely reap it. When a husband lies to his wife he is acting treacherously towards her. God says when a husband acts treacherously towards his wife, He won't regard that husband or readily accept anything from him (see Malachi 2:13-15). If God won't, it's likely the wife won't either. Husbands, if you want your wife to trust you, don't lie to her. If you want your wife to follow you, don't mislead her. If you want your wife to respect you, honor her enough to tell her the truth. It is a big deal.

APPENDIX 2

Wound Care: Dealing With The Aftermath Of The Lie

Time does not heal all wounds. As a matter of fact, depending on the nature and/or severity of the wound, time alone can cause a wound to worsen. Over time, what may appear to be a superficial wound can become infected and lead to death if it is not properly treated. A lie may appear superficial, but it can have devastating consequences in a relationship, especially in marriage. But it does not have to mean the destruction or end of the relationship, or you, if you respond swiftly and appropriately.

If you have been wounded because of a lie or any other form of betrayal, you have cause to be hurt and you have a right to say "Ouch!" To be denied that right or to repress the expression of the pain creates anger and resentment. If it hurts, it hurts. Say "Ouch!" Let the tears flow. God gave us such emotions and the ability to express them for such occasions. Keep in mind, however, that the expression of your hurt and anger is not the same as healing the wound. I have yet to see a wound heal from the wounded person saying ouch. It just doesn't happen. It doesn't matter how loudly you say ouch or how many times you say it, the mere expression of your pain and anger will not bring healing. Let the expression of your hurt and anger serve its purpose which is to let it be known that you have been wounded. But you can't just keep hollering "Ouch!" If you want healing, you have to see to your wound, take whatever precautions you can to protect the wound from further injury and infection, and apply those things that will promote healing.

Appendix 2

Anger has it's place — there are some things that we are supposed to get angry about — but anger, as is true with all of our God-given emotions, must be used appropriately. Anger is like a magnifying glass. When you view things through anger they can appear larger than they really are. When you are dealing with a situation while you are angry, you have to be sure that you are reacting to what is really there and not the distorted or magnified view of what is there. As difficult as it may be, you must take the time, even in your anger, to adjust your "lens" and look at the situation from various angles in order to understand what is really there. In this way, you can use your anger to draw attention where it needs to be and to bring the situation into clearer perspective.

What you apply to your wound can make it better or worse. In the same way, you have to be careful of what you apply to your wound through the magnifying lens of your anger. If you choose to keep rewinding and replaying in your mind the offense that caused the wound instead of pressing the "stop" button; if you spend your time speculating about the unknown and drawing incomplete or false conclusions; if you look for reasons to reinforce your distrust; or if you allow this wound to completely disable the other parts of your relationship that are positive, whole and functioning properly, like rays of sun through a magnifying glass, your anger may burn up and destroy the very thing you are trying to bring into focus — your relationship. You may even burn yourself in the process.

You have limited control over the wounds others may inflict upon you, and to try to control the actions of someone else is an effort in futility. You can set boundaries in place, and take precautionary measures, but you can't stop someone from lying to you or otherwise betraying you. You can, however, control your

Wound Care: Dealing With The Aftermath Of The Lie

own actions and prevent self-inflicted wounds. One of the ways you can wound yourself is by refusing to let go of the offending act. In other words, refusing to forgive. Being unforgiving is like yelling ouch but at the same time poking your finger into your own wound. You're hurting yourself. Unforgiveness is holding on to the very thing that is causing you pain. If someone drops a hot coal in your hand, the best thing to do is drop the hot coal as soon as possible. Why hold onto it and continue to burn yourself? Let it go: the sooner the better. Surrender your control of others and realize the healing power of forgiveness.

Forgiving the one who has wounded you does not mean that you will not remember the offense. You will remember. But when you do remember, remind yourself that you have chosen to forgive. When the negative thoughts come, remind yourself of the things that are right and good also. (If your pool of positive thoughts is limited, this would be a good time to let repetition work for you.) Forgiveness is a process. It is not denying what is wrong; it is acknowledging and holding on to what is right. You forgive for one reason and one reason only: because God has forgiven you. At first you will struggle with forgiving the one who has wounded you because of what was done to you in the past. But as you continue in the process, God will transform your heart because of your obedience to Him, and you will not only be able to forgive past offenses, but you will be able to forgive future offenses... even before they are committed. This is how God forgives us and He instructs us to forgive others in the same way.

Recognize where your strength lies. God is in control and with Him you can face and go through anything! Remember the

Appendix 2

awesome power you have in prayer. Prayer is cathartic. It's like an emotional journal that only God can read and interpret fully and accurately. When you feel the pain, talk to the Divine Doctor. Talk to Him about the kind of wound you received. Talk to Him about the one who wounded you. Talk to Him about your symptoms and side effects: your pain; your disappointment; your anger; your fear. Why worry when you can pray? Worry can't change a thing, but God through prayer can!

This wound hurt you but it didn't kill you and it doesn't have to kill your relationship. Let the phrase, "I shall not surely die" become your daily resolution. If the person who wounded you doesn't change, you shall not surely die! If he leaves, you shall not surely die. If you are wounded again, you shall not surely die! Whatever comes, apply the healing balm of a clear perspective, forgiveness, prayer and courage, and with God's help you can face it, get through it, and be healed!

About the Author

ALEATHEA ANGELA DUPREE

Her first and middle names are literally translated "truth of God messenger." The meaning captures the essence of who she strives to be as a writer, as a counselor, as a minister and as a person. After the publication of her first book, *Though The Vision Tarry: Waiting For My Promised Mate*, there were so many questions and queries for help from her readers, she founded and became the administrator of Deep Waters, a resource website and interactive forum providing biblical answers to relationship issues. Twenty-five plus years as a biblical counselor has helped to equip her as a writer, but it is her own life experiences that qualify her to employ the tools of truth and transparency to transform lives.

Twitter: @CheerUpYourWife
Website: www.cheerupyourwife.info
Facebook: www.facebook.com/cheerupyourwife
Email: cheerupyourwife@dathea.com

Deep Waters Website: www.deepwaters.info
Deep Waters Forum: www.deepwaters.info/forum